THE ART
OF LOVING

By Erich Fromm

THE ART
OF LOVING

ERICH FROMM

PERENNIAL LIBRARY

*Harper & Row, Publishers, New York
Grand Rapids, Philadelphia,
St. Louis, San Francisco, London,
Singapore, Sydney, Tokyo*

This book was originally published in 1956 by Harper & Row, Publishers.

THE ART OF LOVING. Copyright © 1956 by Erich Fromm. All rights reserved. Printed in the United States of America. No part of this book may be used or reproduced in any manner whatsoever without written permission except in the case of brief quotations embodied in critical articles and reviews. For information address Harper & Row, Publishers, Inc., 10 East 53rd Street, New York, N.Y. 10022.

First PERENNIAL LIBRARY edition published 1989.

Designed by Kim Llewellyn

LIBRARY OF CONGRESS CATALOG CARD NUMBER 56-8750

ISBN 0-06-091594-3

95   RRD 20 19 18 17 16 15 14

CONTENTS

FOREWORD

The reading of this book would be a disappointing experience for anyone who expects easy instruction in the art of loving. This book, on the contrary, wants to show that love is not a sentiment which can be easily indulged in by anyone, regardless of the level of maturity reached by him. It wants to convince the reader that all his attempts for love are bound to fail, unless he tries most actively to develop his total personality, so as to achieve a productive orientation; that satisfaction in individual love cannot be attained without the capacity to love one's neighbor, without true humility, courage, faith and discipline. In a culture in which these qualities are rare, the attainment of the capacity to love must remain a rare achievement. Or—anyone can ask himself how many truly loving persons he has known.

Yet, the difficulty of the task must not be a reason to abstain from trying to know the difficulties as well as the conditions for its achievement. To avoid unnecessary complications I have tried to deal with the problem in a language which is non-technical as far as this is possible. For the same reason I have also kept to a minimum references to the literature on love.

For another problem I did not find a completely satisfactory solution; that, namely, of avoiding repetition of ideas expressed in previous books of mine. The reader familiar, especially, with *Escape from Freedom, Man for Himself,* and *The Sane Society,* will find in this book many ideas expressed in these previous works. However, *The Art of Loving* is by no means mainly a recapitulation. It presents many ideas beyond the previously expressed ones, and quite naturally even older ones sometimes gain new perspectives by the fact that they are all centered around one topic, that of the art of loving.

E. F.

He who knows nothing, loves nothing. He who can do nothing understands nothing. He who understands nothing is worthless. But he who understands also loves, notices, sees. . . . The more knowledge is inherent in a thing, the greater the love. . . . Anyone who imagines that all fruits ripen at the same time as the strawberries knows nothing about grapes.

PARACELSUS

I
IS LOVE AN ART?

Is love an art? Then it requires knowledge and effort. Or is love a pleasant sensation, which to experience is a matter of chance, something one "falls into" if one is lucky? This little book is based on the former premise, while undoubtedly the majority of people today believe in the latter.

Not that people think that love is not important. They are starved for it; they watch endless numbers of films about happy and unhappy love stories, they listen to hundreds of trashy songs about love—yet hardly anyone thinks that there is anything that needs to be learned about love.

This peculiar attitude is based on several premises which either singly or combined tend to uphold it. Most people see the problem of love primarily as that of *being loved,* rather than that of *loving,* of one's capacity to love. Hence the problem to them is how to be loved, how to be lovable. In pursuit of this aim they follow several paths. One, which is especially used by men, is to be successful, to be as powerful

1

and rich as the social margin of one's position permits. Another, used especially by women, is to make oneself attractive, by cultivating one's body, dress, etc. Other ways of making oneself attractive, used both by men and women, are to develop pleasant manners, interesting conversation, to be helpful, modest, inoffensive. Many of the ways to make oneself lovable are the same as those used to make oneself successful, "to win friends and influence people." As a matter of fact, what most people in our culture mean by being lovable is essentially a mixture between being popular and having sex appeal.

A second premise behind the attitude that there is nothing to be learned about love is the assumption that the problem of love is the problem of an *object*, not the problem of a *faculty*. People think that to *love* is simple, but that to find the right object to love—or to be loved by—is difficult. This attitude has several reasons rooted in the development of modern society. One reason is the great change which occurred in the twentieth century with respect to the choice of a "love object." In the Victorian age, as in many traditional cultures, love was mostly not a spontaneous personal experience which then might lead to marriage. On the contrary, marriage was contracted by convention—either by the respective families, or by a marriage broker, or without the help of such intermediaries; it was concluded on the basis of social considerations, and love was supposed to develop once the marriage had been concluded. In the last few generations the concept of romantic love has become almost universal in the Western world. In the United States, while considerations of a conventional nature are not entirely absent, to a vast extent people are in search of "romantic love," of the personal experience of love which then should lead to marriage. This new concept of freedom in love must have greatly enhanced the importance of the *object* as against the importance of the *function*.

Closely related to this factor is another feature characteristic of contemporary culture. Our whole culture is based on the appetite for buying, on the idea of a mutually favorable exchange. Modern man's happiness consists in the thrill of looking at the shop windows, and in buying all that he can afford to buy, either for cash or on installments. He (or she) looks at people in a similar way. For the man an attractive girl—and for the woman an attractive man—are the prizes they are after. "Attractive" usually means a nice package of qualities which are popular and sought after on the personality market. What specifically makes a person attractive depends on the fashion of the time, physically as well as mentally. During the twenties, a drinking and smoking girl, tough and sexy, was attractive; today the fashion demands more domesticity and coyness. At the end of the nineteenth and the beginning of this century, a man had to be aggressive and ambitious—today he has to be social and tolerant—in order to be an attractive "package." At any rate, the sense of falling in love develops usually only with regard to such human commodities as are within reach of one's own possibilities for exchange. I am out for a bargain; the object should be desirable from the standpoint of its social value, and at the same time should want me, considering my overt and hidden assets and potentialities. Two persons thus fall in love when they feel they have found the best object available on the market, considering the limitations of their own exchange values. Often, as in buying real estate, the hidden potentialities which can be developed play a considerable role in this bargain. In a culture in which the marketing orientation prevails, and in which material success is the outstanding value, there is little reason to be surprised that human love relations follow the same pattern of exchange which governs the commodity and the labor market.

The third error leading to the assumption that there is nothing to be learned about love lies in the confusion between the initial experience of *"falling"* in love, and the permanent state of *being* in love, or as we might better say, of "standing" in love. If two people who have been strangers, as all of us are, suddenly let the wall between them break down, and feel close, feel one, this moment of oneness is one of the most exhilarating, most exciting experiences in life. It is all the more wonderful and miraculous for persons who have been shut off, isolated, without love. This miracle of sudden intimacy is often facilitated if it is combined with, or initiated by, sexual attraction and consummation. However, this type of love is by its very nature not lasting. The two persons become well acquainted, their intimacy loses more and more its miraculous character, until their antagonism, their disappointments, their mutual boredom kill whatever is left of the initial excitement. Yet, in the beginning they do not know all this: in fact, they take the intensity of the infatuation, this being "crazy" about each other, for proof of the intensity of their love, while it may only prove the degree of their preceding loneliness.

This attitude—that nothing is easier than to love—has continued to be the prevalent idea about love in spite of the overwhelming evidence to the contrary. There is hardly any activity, any enterprise, which is started with such tremendous hopes and expectations, and yet, which fails so regularly, as love. If this were the case with any other activity, people would be eager to know the reasons for the failure, and to learn how one could do better—or they would give up the activity. Since the latter is impossible in the case of love, there seems to be only one adequate way to overcome the failure of love—to examine the reasons for this failure, and to proceed to study the meaning of love.

The first step to take is to become aware that *love is an art*, just as living is an art; if we want to learn how to love we must proceed in the same way we have to proceed if we want to learn any other art, say music, painting, carpentry, or the art of medicine or engineering.

What are the necessary steps in learning any art?

The process of learning an art can be divided conveniently into two parts: one, the mastery of the theory; the other, the mastery of the practice. If I want to learn the art of medicine, I must first know the facts about the human body, and about various diseases. When I have all this theoretical knowledge, I am by no means competent in the art of medicine. I shall become a master in this art only after a great deal of practice, until eventually the results of my theoretical knowledge and the results of my practice are blended into one—my intuition, the essence of the mastery of any art. But, aside from learning the theory and practice, there is a third factor necessary to becoming a master in any art—the mastery of the art must be a matter of ultimate concern; there must be nothing else in the world more important than the art. This holds true for music, for medicine, for carpentry—and for love. And, maybe, here lies the answer to the question of why people in our culture try so rarely to learn this art, in spite of their obvious failures: in spite of the deep-seated craving for love, almost everything else is considered to be more important than love: success, prestige, money, power—almost all our energy is used for the learning of how to achieve these aims, and almost none to learn the art of loving.

Could it be that only those things are considered worthy of being learned with which one can earn money or prestige, and that love, which "only" profits the soul, but is profitless in the modern sense, is a luxury we have no right to spend much energy on? However this may be, the following discussion will treat the art of loving in the sense of the foregoing divisions: first I shall discuss the theory of love—and this will comprise the greater part of the book; and secondly I shall discuss the practice of love—little as can be *said* about practice in this, as in any other field.

II

THE THEORY OF LOVE

I. Love, the Answer to the Problem of Human Existence

Any theory of love must begin with a theory of man, of human existence. While we find love, or rather, the equivalent of love, in animals, their attachments are mainly a part of their instinctual equipment; only remnants of this instinctual equipment can be seen operating in man. What is essential in the existence of man is the fact that he has emerged from the animal kingdom, from instinctive adaptation, that he has transcended nature—although he never leaves it; he is a part of it—and yet once torn away from nature, he cannot return to it; once thrown out of paradise—a state of original oneness with nature—cherubim with flaming swords block his way, if he should try to return. Man can only go forward by developing his reason, by finding a new harmony, a

7

human one, instead of the prehuman harmony which is irretrievably lost.

When man is born, the human race as well as the individual, he is thrown out of a situation which was definite, as definite as the instincts, into a situation which is indefinite, uncertain and open. There is certainty only about the past—and about the future only as far as that it is death.

Man is gifted with reason; he is *life being aware of itself;* he has awareness of himself, of his fellow man, of his past, and of the possibilities of his future. This awareness of himself as a separate entity, the awareness of his own short life span, of the fact that without his will he is born and against his will he dies, that he will die before those whom he loves, or they before him, the awareness of his aloneness and separateness, of his helplessness before the forces of nature and of society, all this makes his separate, disunited existence an unbearable prison. He would become insane could he not liberate himself from this prison and reach out, unite himself in some form or other with men, with the world outside.

The experience of separateness arouses anxiety; it is, indeed, the source of all anxiety. Being separate means being cut off, without any capacity to use my human powers. Hence to be separate means to be helpless, unable to grasp the world—things and people—actively; it means that the world can invade me without my ability to react. Thus, separateness is the source of intense anxiety. Beyond that, it arouses shame and the feeling of guilt. This experience of guilt and shame in separateness is expressed in the Biblical story of Adam and Eve. After Adam and Eve have eaten of the "tree of knowledge of good and evil," after they have disobeyed (there is no good and evil unless there is freedom to disobey), after they have become human by having emancipated themselves from the original animal harmony with nature, i.e., after their birth as human beings—they saw "that they were naked—and they were ashamed." Should we assume that a myth as old and elementary as this has the prudish morals of the nineteenth-century outlook, and that the important point the story wants to convey to us is the embarrassment that their genitals were visible? This can hardly be so, and by understanding the story in a Victorian spirit, we miss the main point, which seems to be the following: after man and woman have become aware of themselves and of each other, they are aware of their separateness, and of their difference, inasmuch as they belong to different sexes. But while recognizing their separateness they remain strangers, because they have not yet learned to love each other (as is also made very clear by the fact that Adam defends himself by blaming Eve, rather than by trying to defend her). *The awareness of human separation, without reunion by love—is the source of shame. It is at the same time the source of guilt and anxiety.*

The deepest need of man, then, is the need to overcome his separateness, to leave the prison of his aloneness. The *absolute* failure to achieve this aim means insanity, because the panic of complete isolation can be overcome only by such a radical withdrawal from the world outside that the feeling of separation disappears—because the world outside, from which one is separated, has disappeared.

Man—of all ages and cultures—is confronted with the solution of one and the same question: the question of how to overcome separateness, how to achieve union, how to transcend one's own individual life and find at-onement. The question is the same for primitive man living in caves, for nomadic man taking care of his flocks, for the peasant in Egypt, the Phoenician trader, the Roman soldier, the medieval monk, the Japanese samurai, the modern clerk and factory hand. The question is the same, for it springs from the same ground: the human situation, the conditions of human existence. The answer varies. The question can be answered by animal worship, by human sacrifice or military conquest, by indulgence in luxury, by ascetic renunciation, by obsessional work, by artistic creation, by the love of God, and by the love of Man. While there are many answers—the record of which is human history—they are nevertheless not innumerable. On the contrary, as soon as one ignores smaller differences which belong more to the periphery than to the center, one discovers that there is only a limited number of answers which have been given, and only could have been given by man in the various cultures in which he has lived. The history of religion and philosophy is the history of these answers, of their diversity, as well as of their limitation in number.

The answers depend, to some extent, on the degree of individuation which an individual has reached. In the infant I-ness has developed but little yet; he still feels one with mother, has no feeling of separateness as long as mother is present. Its sense of aloneness is cured by the physical presence of the mother, her breasts, her skin. Only to the degree that the child develops his sense of separateness and individuality is the physical presence of the mother not sufficient any more, and does the need to overcome separateness in other ways arise.

Similarly, the human race in its infancy still feels one with nature. The soil, the animals, the plants are still man's world. He identifies himself with animals, and this is expressed by the wearing of animal masks, by the worshiping of a totem animal or animal gods. But the more the human race emerges from these primary bonds, the more it separates itself from the natural world, the more intense becomes the need to find new ways of escaping separateness.

One way of achieving this aim lies in all kinds of *orgiastic states*. These may have the form of an auto-induced trance, sometimes with the help of drugs. Many rituals of primitive tribes offer a vivid picture of this type of solution. In a transitory state of exaltation the world outside disappears, and with it the feeling of separateness from it. Inasmuch as these rituals are practiced in common, an experience of fusion with the group is added which makes this solution all the more effective. Closely related to, and often blended with this orgiastic solution, is the sexual experience. The sexual orgasm can produce a state similar to the one produced by a trance, or to the effects of certain drugs. Rites of communal sexual orgies were a part of many primitive rituals. It seems that after the orgiastic experience, man can go on for a time without suffering too much from his separateness. Slowly the tension of anxiety mounts, and then is reduced again by the repeated performance of the ritual.

As long as these orgiastic states are a matter of common practice in a tribe, they do not produce anxiety or guilt. To act in this way is right, and even virtuous, because it is a way shared by all, approved and demanded by the medicine men or priests; hence there is no reason to feel guilty or ashamed. It is quite different when the same solution is chosen by an individual in a culture which has left behind these common practices. Alcoholism and drug addiction are the forms which the individual chooses in a non-orgiastic culture. In contrast to those participating in the socially patterned solution, such individuals suffer from guilt feelings and remorse. While they try to escape from separateness by taking refuge in alcohol or drugs, they feel all the more separate after the orgiastic experience is over, and thus are driven to take recourse to it with increasing frequency and intensity. Slightly different from this is the recourse to a sexual orgiastic solution. To some extent it is a natural and normal form of overcoming separateness, and a partial answer to the problem of isolation. But in many individuals in whom separateness is not relieved in other ways, the search for the sexual orgasm assumes a function which makes it not very different from alcoholism and drug addiction. It becomes a desperate attempt to escape the anxiety engendered by separateness, and it results in an ever-increasing sense of separateness, since the sexual act without love never bridges the gap between two human beings, except momentarily.

All forms of orgiastic union have three characteristics: they are intense, even violent; they occur in the total personality, mind *and* body; they are transitory and periodical. Exactly the opposite holds true for that form of union which is by far the most frequent solution chosen by man in the past and in the present: the union based on *conformity* with the group, its customs, practices and beliefs. Here again we find a considerable development.

In a primitive society the group is small; it consists of those with whom one shares blood and soil. With the growing development of culture, the group enlarges; it becomes the citizenry of a *polis,* the citizenry of a large state, the members of a church. Even the poor Roman felt pride because he could say *"civis romanus sum";* Rome and the Empire were his family, his home, his world. Also in contemporary Western society the union with the group is the prevalent way of overcoming separateness. It is a union in which the individual self disappears to a large extent, and where the aim is to belong to the herd. If I am like everybody else, if I have no feelings or thoughts which make me different, if I conform in custom, dress, ideas, to the pattern of the group, I am saved; saved from the frightening experience of aloneness. The dictatorial systems use threats and terror to induce this conformity; the democratic countries, suggestion and propaganda. There is, indeed, one great difference between the two systems. In the democracies non-conformity is possible and, in fact, by no means entirely absent; in the totalitarian systems, only a few unusual heroes and martyrs can be expected to refuse obedience. But in spite of this difference the democratic societies show an overwhelming degree of conformity. The reason lies in the fact that there *has* to be an answer to the quest for union, and if there is no other or better way, then the union of herd conformity becomes the predominant one. One can only understand the power of the fear to be different, the fear to be only a few steps away from the herd, if one understands the depths of the need not to be separated. Sometimes this fear of non-conformity is rationalized as fear of practical dangers which could threaten the non-conformist. But actually, people *want* to conform to a much higher degree than they are *forced* to conform, at least in the Western democracies.

Most people are not even aware of their need to conform. They live under the illusion that they follow their own ideas and inclinations, that they are individualists, that they have arrived at their opinions as the result of their own thinking—and that it just happens that their ideas are the same as those of the majority. The consensus of all serves as a proof for the correctness of "their" ideas. Since there is still a need to feel some individuality, such need is satisfied with regard to minor differences; the initials on the handbag or the sweater, the name plate of the bank teller, the belonging to the Democratic as against the Republican party, to the Elks instead of to the Shriners become the expression of individual differences. The advertising slogan of "it is different" shows up this pathetic need for difference, when in reality there is hardly any left.

This increasing tendency for the elimination of differences is closely related to the concept and the experience of equality, as it is developing in the most advanced industrial societies. Equality had meant, in a religious context, that we are all God's children, that we all share in the same human-

divine substance, that we are all one. It meant also that the
very differences between individuals must be respected, that
while it is true that we are all one, it is also true that each one
of us is a unique entity, is a cosmos by itself. Such conviction
of the uniqueness of the individual is expressed for instance
in the Talmudic statement: "Whosoever saves a single life is
as if he had saved the whole world; whosoever destroys a
single life is as if he had destroyed the whole world." Equality
as a condition for the development of individuality was also
the meaning of the concept in the philosophy of the Western
Enlightenment. It meant (most clearly formulated by Kant)
that no man must be the means for the ends of another man.
That all men are equal inasmuch as they are ends, and only
ends, and never means to each other. Following the ideas of
the Enlightenment, Socialist thinkers of various schools defined equality as abolition of exploitation, of the use of man
by man, regardless of whether this use were cruel or
"human."

In contemporary capitalistic society the meaning of equality has been transformed. By equality one refers to the equality of automatons; of men who have lost their individuality.
Equality today means "sameness," rather than "oneness." It
is the sameness of abstractions, of the men who work in the
same jobs, who have the same amusements, who read the
same newspapers, who have the same feelings and the same
ideas. In this respect one must also look with some skepticism
at some achievements which are usually praised as signs of
our progress, such as the equality of women. Needless to say
I am not speaking against the equality of women; but the
positive aspects of this tendency for equality must not deceive one. It is part of the trend toward the elimination of
differences. Equality is bought at this very price: women are
equal because they are not different any more. The proposition of Enlightenment philosophy, *l'âme n'a pas de sexe,* the

soul has no sex, has become the general practice. The polarity of the sexes is disappearing, and with it erotic love, which is based on this polarity. Men and women become the *same,* not *equals* as opposite poles. Contemporary society preaches this ideal of unindividualized equality because it needs human atoms, each one the same, to make them function in a mass aggregation, smoothly, without friction; all obeying the same commands, yet everybody being convinced that he is following his own desires. Just as modern mass production requires the standardization of commodities, so the social process requires standardization of man, and this standardization is called "equality."

Union by conformity is not intense and violent; it is calm, dictated by routine, and for this very reason often is insufficient to pacify the anxiety of separateness. The incidence of alcoholism, drug addiction, compulsive sexualism, and suicide in contemporary Western society are symptoms of this relative failure of herd conformity. Furthermore, this solution concerns mainly the mind and not the body, and for this reason too is lacking in comparison with the orgiastic solutions. Herd conformity has only one advantage: it is permanent, and not spasmodic. The individual is introduced into the conformity pattern at the age of three or four, and subsequently never loses his contact with the herd. Even his funeral, which he anticipates as his last great social affair, is in strict conformance with the pattern.

In addition to conformity as a way to relieve the anxiety springing from separateness, another factor of contemporary life must be considered: the role of the work routine and of the pleasure routine. Man becomes a "nine to fiver," he is part of the labor force, or the bureaucratic force of clerks and managers. He has little initiative, his tasks are prescribed by the organization of the work; there is even little difference between those high up on the ladder and those on the bottom. They all perform tasks prescribed by the whole structure of the organization, at a prescribed speed, and in a prescribed manner. Even the feelings are prescribed: cheerfulness, tolerance, reliability, ambition, and an ability to get along with everybody without friction. Fun is routinized in similar, although not quite as drastic ways. Books are selected by the book clubs, movies by the film and theater owners and the advertising slogans paid for by them; the rest is also uniform: the Sunday ride in the car, the television session, the card game, the social parties. From birth to death, from Monday to Monday, from morning to evening—all activities are routinized, and prefabricated. How should a man caught in this net of routine not forget that he is a man, a unique individual, one who is given only this one chance of living, with hopes and disappointments, with sorrow and fear, with the longing for love and the dread of the nothing and of separateness?

A third way of attaining union lies in *creative activity*, be it that of the artist, or of the artisan. In any kind of creative work the creating person unites himself with his material, which represents the world outside of himself. Whether a carpenter makes a table, or a goldsmith a piece of jewelry, whether the peasant grows his corn, or the painter paints a picture, in all types of creative work the worker and his object become one, man unites himself with the world in the process of creation. This, however, holds true only for productive work, for work in which *I* plan, produce, see the result of my work. In the modern work process of a clerk, the worker on the endless belt, little is left of this uniting quality of work. The worker becomes an appendix to the machine or to the bureaucratic organization. He has ceased to be he—hence no union takes place beyond that of conformity.

The unity achieved in productive work is not interpersonal; the unity achieved in orgiastic fusion is transitory; the unity achieved by conformity is only pseudo-unity. Hence, they are only partial answers to the problem of existence. The full answer lies in the achievement of interpersonal union, of fusion with another person, in *love*. STOP

This desire for interpersonal fusion is the most powerful striving in man. It is the most fundamental passion, it is the force which keeps the human race together, the clan, the family, society. The failure to achieve it means insanity or destruction—self-destruction or destruction of others. Without love, humanity could not exist for a day. Yet, if we call the achievement of interpersonal union "love," we find ourselves in a serious difficulty. Fusion can be achieved in different ways—and the differences are not less significant than what is common to the various forms of love. Should they all be called love? Or should we reserve the word "love" only for a specific kind of union, one which has been the ideal virtue in all great humanistic religions and philosophical systems of the last four thousand years of Western and Eastern history?

As with all semantic difficulties, the answer can only be arbitrary. What matters is that we know what kind of union we are talking about when we speak of love. Do we refer to love as the mature answer to the problem of existence, or do we speak of those immature forms of love which may be called *symbiotic union?* In the following pages I shall call love only the former. I shall begin the discussion of "love" with the latter.

Symbiotic union has its biological pattern in the relationship between the pregnant mother and the foetus. They are two, and yet one. They live "together" *(sym-biosis),* they need each other. The foetus is a part of the mother, it receives everything it needs from her; mother is its world, as it were; she feeds it, she protects it, but also her own life is enhanced by it. In the *psychic* symbiotic union, the two bodies are independent, but the same kind of attachment exists psychologically.

The *passive* form of the symbiotic union is that of submission, or if we use a clinical term, of *masochism*. The masochistic person escapes from the unbearable feeling of isolation and separateness by making himself part and parcel of another person who directs him, guides him, protects him; who is his life and his oxygen, as it were. The power of the one to whom one submits is inflated, may he be a person or a god; he is everything, I am nothing, except inasmuch as I am part of him. As a part, I am part of greatness, of power, of certainty. The masochistic person does not have to make decisions, does not have to take any risks; he is never alone—but he is not independent; he has no integrity; he is not yet fully born. In a religious context the object of worship is called an idol; in a secular context of a masochistic love relationship the essential mechanism, that of idolatry, is the same. The masochistic relationship can be blended with physical, sexual desire; in this case it is not only a submission in which one's mind participates, but also one's whole body. There can be masochistic submission to fate, to sickness, to rhythmic music, to the orgiastic state produced by drugs or under hypnotic trance—in all these instances the person renounces his integrity, makes himself the instrument of somebody or something outside of himself; he need not solve the problem of living by productive activity.

The *active* form of symbiotic fusion is domination or, to use the psychological term corresponding to masochism, *sadism*. The sadistic person wants to escape from his aloneness and his sense of imprisonment by making another person part and parcel of himself. He inflates and enhances himself by incorporating another person, who worships him.

The sadistic person is as dependent on the submissive person as the latter is on the former; neither can live without the other. The difference is only that the sadistic person commands, exploits, hurts, humiliates, and that the masochistic person is commanded, exploited, hurt, humiliated. This is a considerable difference in a realistic sense; in a deeper emotional sense, the difference is not so great as that which they both have in common: fusion without integrity. If one understands this, it is also not surprising to find that usually a person reacts in both the sadistic and the masochistic manner, usually toward different objects. Hitler reacted primarily in a sadistic fashion toward people, but masochistically toward fate, history, the "higher power" of nature. His end—suicide among general destruction—is as characteristic as was his dream of success—total domination.[1]

In contrast to symbiotic union, mature *love* is *union under the condition of preserving one's integrity,* one's individuality. *Love is an active power in man;* a power which breaks through the walls which separate man from his fellow men, which unites him with others; love makes him overcome the sense of isolation and separateness, yet it permits him to be himself, to retain his integrity. In love the paradox occurs that two beings become one and yet remain two.

If we say love is an activity, we face a difficulty which lies in the ambiguous meaning of the word "activity." By "activity," in the modern usage of the word, is usually meant an action which brings about a change in an existing situation by means of an expenditure of energy. Thus a man is considered active if he does business, studies medicine, works on an endless belt, builds a table, or is engaged in sports. Common to all these activities is that they are directed toward an outside goal to be achieved. What is *not* taken into account is the *motivation* of activity. Take for instance a man driven

[1] Cf. a more detailed study of sadism and masochism in E. Fromm, *Escape from Freedom,* Rinehart & Company, New York, 1941.

to incessant work by a sense of deep insecurity and loneliness; or another one driven by ambition, or greed for money. In all these cases the person is the slave of a passion, and his activity is in reality a "passivity" because he is driven; he is the sufferer, not the "actor." On the other hand, a man sitting quiet and contemplating, with no purpose or aim except that of experiencing himself and his oneness with the world, is considered to be "passive," because he is not "doing" anything. In reality, this attitude of concentrated meditation is the highest activity there is, an activity of the soul, which is possible only under the condition of inner freedom and independence. One concept of activity, the modern one, refers to the use of energy for the achievement of external aims; the other concept of activity refers to the use of man's inherent powers, regardless of whether any external change is brought about. The latter concept of activity has been formulated most clearly by Spinoza. He differentiates among the affects between active and passive affects, "actions" and "passions." In the exercise of an active affect, man is free, he is the master of his affect; in the exercise of a passive affect, man is driven, the object of motivations of which he himself is not aware. Thus Spinoza arrives at the statement that virtue and power are one and the same.[2] Envy, jealousy, ambition, any kind of greed are passions; love is an action, the practice of a human power, which can be practiced only in freedom and never as the result of a compulsion.

Love is an activity, not a passive affect; it is a "standing in," not a "falling for." In the most general way, the active character of love can be described by stating that love is primarily *giving*, not receiving.

What is giving? Simple as the answer to this question seems to be, it is actually full of ambiguities and complexities. The

[2]Spinoza, *Ethics* IV, Def. 8.

most widespread misunderstanding is that which assumes that giving is "giving up" something, being deprived of, sacrificing. The person whose character has not developed beyond the stage of the receptive, exploitative, or hoarding orientation, experiences the act of giving in this way. The marketing character is willing to give, but only in exchange for receiving; giving without receiving for him is being cheated.[3] People whose main orientation is a non-productive one feel giving as an impoverishment. Most individuals of this type therefore refuse to give. Some make a virtue out of giving in the sense of a sacrifice. They feel that just because it is painful to give, one *should* give; the virtue of giving to them lies in the very act of acceptance of the sacrifice. For them, the norm that it is better to give than to receive means that it is better to suffer deprivation than to experience joy.

For the productive character, giving has an entirely different meaning. Giving is the highest expression of potency. In the very act of giving, I experience my strength, my wealth, my power. This experience of heightened vitality and potency fills me with joy. I experience myself as overflowing, spending, alive, hence as joyous.[4] Giving is more joyous than receiving, not because it is a deprivation, but because in the act of giving lies the expression of my aliveness.

It is not difficult to recognize the validity of this principle by applying it to various specific phenomena. The most elementary example lies in the sphere of sex. The culmination of the male sexual function lies in the act of giving; the man gives himself, his sexual organ, to the woman. At the moment of orgasm he gives his semen to her. He cannot help giving

[3]Cf. a detailed discussion of these character orientations in E. Fromm, *Man for Himself,* Rinehart & Company, New York, 1947, Chap. III, pp. 54–117.

[4]Compare the definition of joy given by Spinoza.

it if he is potent. If he cannot give, he is impotent. For the woman the process is not different, although somewhat more complex. She gives herself too; she opens the gates to her feminine center; in the act of receiving, she gives. If she is incapable of this act of giving, if she can only receive, she is frigid. With her the act of giving occurs again, not in her function as a lover, but in that as a mother. She gives of herself to the growing child within her, she gives her milk to the infant, she gives her bodily warmth. Not to give would be painful.

In the sphere of material things giving means being rich. Not he who *has* much is rich, but he who *gives* much. The hoarder who is anxiously worried about losing something is, psychologically speaking, the poor, impoverished man, regardless of how much he has. Whoever is capable of giving of himself is rich. He experiences himself as one who can confer of himself to others. Only one who is deprived of all that goes beyond the barest necessities for subsistence would be incapable of enjoying the act of giving material things. But daily experience shows that what a person considers the minimal necessities depends as much on his character as it depends on his actual possessions. It is well known that the poor are more willing to give than the rich. Nevertheless, poverty beyond a certain point may make it impossible to give, and is so degrading, not only because of the suffering it causes directly, but because of the fact that it deprives the poor of the joy of giving.

The most important sphere of giving, however, is not that of material things, but lies in the specifically human realm. What does one person give to another? He gives of himself, of the most precious he has, he gives of his life. This does not necessarily mean that he sacrifices his life for the other—but that he gives him of that which is alive in him; he gives him of his joy, of his interest, of his understanding, of his knowledge, of his humor, of his sadness—of all expressions and manifestations of that which is alive in him. In thus giving of his life, he enriches the other person, he enhances the other's sense of aliveness by enhancing his own sense of aliveness. He does not give in order to receive; giving is in itself exquisite joy. But in giving he cannot help bringing something to life in the other person, and this which is brought to life reflects back to him; in truly giving, he cannot help receiving that which is given back to him. Giving implies to make the other person a giver also and they both share in the joy of what they have brought to life. In the act of giving something is born, and both persons involved are grateful for the life that is born for both of them. Specifically with regard to love this means: love is a power which produces love; impotence is the inability to produce love. This thought has been beautifully expressed by Marx: "Assume," he says, "*man* as *man,* and his relation to the world as a human one, and you can exchange love only for love, confidence for confidence, etc. If you wish to enjoy art, you must be an artistically trained person; if you wish to have influence on other people, you must be a person who has a really stimulating and furthering influence on other people. Every one of your relationships to man and to nature must be a definite expression of your *real, individual* life corresponding to the object of your will. If you love without calling forth love, that is, if your love as such does not produce love, if by means of an *expression of life* as a loving person you do not make of yourself a *loved person,* then your love is impotent, a misfortune."[5] But not only in love does giving mean receiving. The teacher is taught by his students, the actor is stimulated by his audience, the psycho-

[5]"Nationalökonomie und Philosophie," 1844, published in Karl Marx' *Die Frühschriften,* Alfred Kröner Verlag, Stuttgart, 1953, pp. 300, 301. (My translation. E. F.)

analyst is cured by his patient—provided they do not treat each other as objects, but are related to each other genuinely and productively.

It is hardly necessary to stress the fact that the ability to love as an act of giving depends on the character development of the person. It presupposes the attainment of a predominantly productive orientation; in this orientation the person has overcome dependency, narcissistic omnipotence, the wish to exploit others, or to hoard, and has acquired faith in his own human powers, courage to rely on his powers in the attainment of his goals. To the degree that these qualities are lacking, he is afraid of giving himself—hence of loving.

Beyond the element of giving, the active character of love becomes evident in the fact that it always implies certain basic elements, common to all forms of love. These are *care, responsibility, respect* and *knowledge.*

That love implies *care* is most evident in a mother's love for her child. No assurance of her love would strike us as sincere if we saw her lacking in care for the infant, if she neglected to feed it, to bathe it, to give it physical comfort; and we are impressed by her love if we see her caring for the child. It is not different even with the love for animals or flowers. If a woman told us that she loved flowers, and we saw that she forgot to water them, we would not believe in her "love" for flowers. *Love is the active concern for the life and the growth of that which we love.* Where this active concern is lacking, there is no love. This element of love has been beautifully described in the book of Jonah. God has told Jonah to go to Nineveh to warn its inhabitants that they will be punished unless they mend their evil ways. Jonah runs away from his mission because he is afraid that the people of Nineveh will repent and that God will forgive them. He is a man with a strong sense of order and law, but without love. However, in his attempt to escape, he finds himself in the belly of a whale, symbolizing the state of isolation and imprisonment which his lack of love and solidarity has brought upon him. God saves him, and Jonah goes to Nineveh. He preaches to the inhabitants as God had told him, and the very thing he was afraid of happens. The men of Nineveh repent their sins, mend their ways, and God forgives them and decides not to destroy the city. Jonah is intensely angry and disappointed; he wanted "justice" to be done, not mercy. At last he finds some comfort in the shade of a tree which God had made to grow for him to protect him from the sun. But when God makes the tree wilt, Jonah is depressed and angrily complains to God. God answers: "Thou hast had pity on the gourd for the which thou hast not labored neither madest it grow; which came up in a night, and perished in a night. And should I not spare Nineveh, that great city, wherein are more than sixscore thousand people that cannot discern between their right hand and their left hand; and also much cattle?" God's answer to Jonah is to be understood symbolically. God explains to Jonah that the essence of love is to "labor" for something and "to make something grow," that love and labor are inseparable. One loves that for which one labors, and one labors for that which one loves.

Care and concern imply another aspect of love; that of *responsibility*. Today responsibility is often meant to denote duty, something imposed upon one from the outside. But responsibility, in its true sense, is an entirely voluntary act; it is my response to the needs, expressed or unexpressed, of another human being. To be "responsible" means to be able and ready to "respond." Jonah did not feel responsible to the inhabitants of Nineveh. He, like Cain, could ask: "Am I my brother's keeper?" The loving person responds. The life of his brother is not his brother's business alone, but his own. He feels responsible for his fellow men, as he feels responsible for himself. This responsibility, in the case of the mother and her infant, refers mainly to the care for physical needs. In the love between adults it refers mainly to the psychic needs of the other person.

Responsibility could easily deteriorate into domination and possessiveness, were it not for a third component of love, *respect*. Respect is not fear and awe; it denotes, in accordance with the root of the word (*respicere* = to look at), the ability to see a person as he is, to be aware of his unique individuality. Respect means the concern that the other person should grow and unfold as he is. Respect, thus, implies the absence of exploitation. I want the loved person to grow and unfold for his own sake, and in his own ways, and not for the purpose of serving me. If I love the other person, I feel one with him or her, but with him *as he is,* not as I need him to be as an object for my use. It is clear that respect is possible only if *I* have achieved independence; if I can stand and walk without needing crutches, without having to dominate and exploit anyone else. Respect exists only on the basis of freedom: *"l'amour est l'enfant de la liberté"* as an old French song says; love is the child of freedom, never that of domination.

To respect a person is not possible without *knowing* him; care and responsibility would be blind if they were not guided by knowledge. Knowledge would be empty if it were not motivated by concern. There are many layers of knowledge; the knowledge which is an aspect of love is one which does not stay at the periphery, but penetrates to the core. It is possible only when I can transcend the concern for myself and see the other person in his own terms. I may know, for instance, that a person is angry, even if he does not show it overtly; but I may know him more deeply than that; then I know that he is anxious, and worried; that he feels lonely, that he feels guilty. Then I know that his anger is only the manifestation of something deeper, and I see him as anxious and embarrassed, that is, as the suffering person, rather than as the angry one.

Knowledge has one more, and a more fundamental, relation to the problem of love. The basic need to fuse with another person so as to transcend the prison of one's separateness is closely related to another specifically human desire, that to know the "secret of man." While life in its merely biological aspects is a miracle and a secret, man in his human aspects is an unfathomable secret to himself—and to his fellow man. We know ourselves, and yet even with all the efforts we may make, we do not know ourselves. We know our fellow man, and yet we do not know him, because we are not a thing, and our fellow man is not a thing. The further we reach into the depth of our being, or someone else's being, the more the goal of knowledge eludes us. Yet we cannot help desiring to penetrate into the secret of man's soul, into the innermost nucleus which is "he."

There is one way, a desperate one, to know the secret: it is that of complete power over another person; the power which makes him do what we want, feel what we want, think what we want; which transforms him into a thing, our thing, our possession. The ultimate degree of this attempt to know lies in the extremes of sadism, the desire and ability to make a human being suffer; to torture him, to force him to betray his secret in his suffering. In this craving for penetrating man's secret, his and hence our own, lies an essential motivation for the depth and intensity of cruelty and destructiveness. In a very succinct way this idea has been expressed by Isaac Babel. He quotes a fellow officer in the Russian civil war, who has just stamped his former master to death, as saying: "With shooting—I'll put it this way—with shooting you only get rid of a chap. . . . With shooting you'll never get at the soul, to where it is in a fellow and how it shows itself. But I don't spare myself, and I've more than once trampled an enemy for over an hour. You see, I want to get to know what life really is, what life's like down our way."[6]

In children we often see this path to knowledge quite overtly. The child takes something apart, breaks it up in order to know it; or it takes an animal apart; cruelly tears off the wings of a butterfly in order to know it, to force its secret. The cruelty itself is motivated by something deeper: the wish to know the secret of things and of life.

The other path to knowing "the secret" is love. Love is active penetration of the other person, in which my desire to know is stilled by union. In the act of fusion I know you, I know myself, I know everybody—and I "know" nothing. I know in the only way knowledge of that which is alive is possible for man—by experience of union—not by any knowledge our thought can give. Sadism is motivated by the wish to know the secret, yet I remain as ignorant as I was before. I have torn the other being apart limb from limb, yet all I have done is to destroy him. Love is the only way of knowledge, which in the act of union answers my quest. In the act of loving, of giving myself, in the act of penetrating the other person, I find myself, I discover myself, I discover us both, I discover man.

The longing to know ourselves and to know our fellow man has been expressed in the Delphic motto "Know thyself." It is the mainspring of all psychology. But inasmuch as the desire is to know all of man, his innermost secret, the desire can never be fulfilled in knowledge of the ordinary kind, in knowledge only by thought. Even if we knew a thousand times more of ourselves, we would never reach bottom. We would still remain an enigma to ourselves, as our fellow man would remain an enigma to us. The only way of full knowledge lies in the *act* of love: this act transcends thought, it

[6] I. Babel, *The Collected Stories*, Criterion Book, New York, 1955.

transcends words. It is the daring plunge into the experience of union. However, knowledge in thought, that is psychological knowledge, is a necessary condition for full knowledge in the act of love. I have to know the other person and myself objectively, in order to be able to see his reality, or rather, to overcome the illusions, the irrationally distorted picture I have of him. Only if I know a human being objectively, can I know him in his ultimate essence, in the act of love.[7]

/The problem of knowing man is parallel to the religious problem of knowing God./In conventional Western theology the attempt is made to know God by thought, to make statements *about* God. It is assumed that I can know God in my thought. In mysticism, which is the consequent outcome of monotheism (as I shall try to show later on), the attempt is given up to know God by thought, and it is replaced by the experience of union with God in which there is no more room—and no need—for knowledge *about* God.

The experience of union, with man, or religiously speaking, with God, is by no means irrational. On the contrary, it is as Albert Schweitzer has pointed out, the consequence of rationalism, its most daring and radical consequence. It is based on our knowledge of the fundamental, and not accidental, limitations of our knowledge. It is the knowledge that we shall never "grasp" the secret of man and of the universe, but that we can know, nevertheless, in the act of love. Psychology as a science has its limitations, and, as the logical consequence of theology is mysticism, so the ultimate consequence of psychology is love.

---

[7]The above statement has an important implication for the role of psychology in contemporary Western culture. While the great popularity of psychology certainly indicates an interest in the knowledge of man, it also betrays the fundamental lack of love in human relations today. Psychological knowledge thus becomes a substitute for full knowledge in the act of love, instead of being a step toward it.

Care, responsibility, respect and knowledge are mutually interdependent. They are a syndrome of attitudes which are to be found in the mature person; that is, in the person who develops his own powers productively, who only wants to have that which he has worked for, who has given up narcissistic dreams of omniscience and omnipotence, who has acquired humility based on the inner strength which only genuine productive activity can give.

Thus far I have spoken of love as the overcoming of human separateness, as the fulfillment of the longing for union. But above the universal, existential need for union rises a more specific, biological one: the desire for union between the masculine and feminine poles. The idea of this polarization is most strikingly expressed in the myth that originally man and woman were one, that they were cut in half, and from then on each male has been seeking for the lost female part of himself in order to unite again with her. (The same idea of the original unity of the sexes is also contained in the Biblical story of Eve being made from Adam's rib, even though in this story, in the spirit of patriarchalism, woman is considered secondary to man.) The meaning of the myth is clear enough. Sexual polarization leads man to seek union in a specific way, that of union with the other sex. The polarity between the male and female principles exists also *within* each man and each woman. Just as physiologically man and woman each have hormones of the opposite sex, they are bisexual also in the psychological sense. They carry in themselves the principle of receiving and of penetrating, of matter and of spirit. Man—and woman—finds union within himself only in the union of his female and his male polarity. This polarity is the basis for all creativity.

The male-female polarity is also the basis for interpersonal creativity. This is obvious biologically in the fact that the union of sperm and ovum is the basis for the birth of a child. But in the purely psychic realm it is not different; in the love between man and woman, each of them is reborn. (The homosexual deviation is a failure to attain this polarized union, and thus the homosexual suffers from the pain of never-resolved separateness; a failure, however, which he shares with the average heterosexual who cannot love.)

The same polarity of the male and female principle exists in nature; not only, as is obvious in animals and plants, but in the polarity of the two fundamental functions, that of receiving and that of penetrating. It is the polarity of the earth and rain, of the river and the ocean, of night and day, of darkness and light, of matter and spirit. This idea is beautifully expressed by the great Muslim poet and mystic, Rūmī:

Never, in sooth, does the lover seek without being sought
    by his beloved.
When the lightning of love has shot into *this* heart, know
    that there is love in *that* heart.
When love of God waxes in thy heart, beyond any doubt
    God hath love for thee.
No sound of clapping comes from one hand without the
    other hand.
Divine Wisdom is destiny and decree made us lovers of one
    another.
Because of that fore-ordainment every part of the world is
    paired with its mate.
In the view of the wise, Heaven is man and Earth woman:
    Earth fosters what Heaven lets fall.
When Earth lacks heat, Heaven sends it; when she has lost
    her freshness and moisture, Heaven restores it.
Heaven goes on his rounds, like a husband foraging for the
    wife's sake;

And Earth is busy with housewiferies: she attends to births
and suckling that which she bears.
Regard Earth and Heaven as endowed with intelligence,
since they do the work of intelligent beings.
Unless these twain taste pleasure from one another, why
are they creeping together like sweethearts?
Without the Earth, how should flower and tree blossom?
What, then, would Heaven's water and heat produce?
As God put desire in man and woman to the end that the
world should be preserved by their union,
So hath He implanted in every part of existence the desire
for another part.
Day and Night are enemies outwardly; yet both serve one
purpose,
Each in love with the other for the sake of perfecting their
mutual work,
Without Night, the nature of Man would receive no
income, so there would be nothing for Day to spend.[8]

The problem of the male-female polarity leads to some
further discussion on the subject matter of love and sex. I
have spoken before of Freud's error in seeing in love exclusively the expression—or a sublimation—of the sexual instinct, rather than recognizing that the sexual desire is one
manifestation of the need for love and union. But Freud's
error goes deeper. In line with his physiological materialism,
he sees in the sexual instinct the result of a chemically produced tension in the body which is painful and seeks for
relief. The aim of the sexual desire is the removal of this
painful tension; sexual satisfaction lies in the accomplishment

[8]R. A. Nicholson, *Rūmī,* George Allen and Unwin, Ltd., London, 1950, pp.
122–3.

of this removal. This view has its validity to the extent that the sexual desire operates in the same fashion as hunger or thirst do when the organism is undernourished. Sexual desire, in this concept, is an itch, sexual satisfaction the removal of the itch. In fact, as far as this concept of sexuality is concerned, masturbation would be the ideal sexual satisfaction. What Freud, paradoxically enough, ignores, is the psycho-biological aspect of sexuality, the masculine-feminine polarity, and the desire to bridge this polarity by union. This curious error was probably facilitated by Freud's extreme patriarchalism, which led him to the assumption that sexuality per se is masculine, and thus made him ignore the specific female sexuality. He expressed this idea in the *Three Contributions to the Theory of Sex,* saying that the libido has regularly "a masculine nature," regardless of whether it is the libido in a man or in a woman. The same idea is also expressed in a rationalized form in Freud's theory that the little boy experiences the woman as a castrated man, and that she herself seeks for various compensations for the loss of the male genital. But woman is not a castrated man, and her sexuality is specifically feminine and not of "a masculine nature."

Sexual attraction between the sexes is only partly motivated by the need for removal of tension; it is mainly the need for union with the other sexual pole. In fact, erotic attraction is by no means only expressed in sexual attraction. There is masculinity and femininity in *character* as well as in *sexual function.* The masculine character can be defined as having the qualities of penetration, guidance, activity, discipline and adventurousness; the feminine character by the qualities of productive receptiveness, protection, realism, endurance, motherliness. (It must always be kept in mind that in each individual both characteristics are blended, but with the pre-

ponderance of those appertaining to "his" or "her" sex.) Very
often if the masculine *character* traits of a man are weakened
because emotionally he has remained a child, he will try to
compensate for this lack by the exclusive emphasis on his
male role in *sex*. The result is the Don Juan, who needs to
prove his male prowess in sex because he is unsure of his
masculinity in a characterological sense. When the paralysis
of masculinity is more extreme, sadism (the use of force)
becomes the main—a perverted—substitute for masculinity.
If the feminine sexuality is weakened or perverted, it is transformed into masochism, or possessiveness.

Freud has been criticized for his overevaluation of sex.
This criticism was often prompted by the wish to remove an
element from Freud's system which aroused criticism and
hostility among conventionally minded people. Freud
keenly sensed this motivation and for this very reason fought
every attempt to change his theory of sex. Indeed, in his
time, Freud's theory had a challenging and revolutionary
character. But what was true around 1900 is not true any
more fifty years later. The sexual mores have changed so
much that Freud's theories are not any longer shocking to
the Western middle classes, and it is a quixotic kind of radicalism when orthodox analysts today still think they are courageous and radical in defending Freud's sexual theory. In
fact, their brand of psychoanalysis is conformist, and does not
try to raise psychological questions which would lead to a
criticism of contemporary society.

My criticism of Freud's theory is not that he overempha-
sized sex, but his failure to understand sex deeply enough.
He took the first step in discovering the significance of interpersonal passions; in accordance with his philosophic premises he explained them physiologically. In the further development of psychoanalysis it is necessary to correct and
deepen Freud's concept by translating Freud's insights from

the physiological into the biological and existential dimension.[9]

2. Love Between Parent and Child

The infant, at the moment of birth, would feel the fear of dying, if a gracious fate did not preserve it from any awareness of the anxiety involved in the separation from mother, and from intra-uterine existence. Even after being born, the infant is hardly different from what it was before birth; it cannot recognize objects, it is not yet aware of itself, and of the world as being outside of itself. It only feels the positive stimulation of warmth and food, and it does not yet differentiate warmth and food from its source: mother. Mother *is* warmth, mother *is* food, mother *is* the euphoric state of satisfaction and security. This state is one of narcissism, to use Freud's term. The outside reality, persons and things, have meaning only in terms of their satisfying or frustrating the inner state of the body. Real is only what is within; what is outside is real only in terms of my needs—never in terms of its own qualities or needs.

When the child grows and develops, he becomes capable of perceiving things as they are; the satisfaction in being fed becomes differentiated from the nipple, the breast from the mother. Eventually the child experiences his thirst, the satisfying milk, the breast and the mother, as different entities. He learns to perceive many other things as being different,

[9]Freud himself made a first step in this direction in his later concept of the life and death instincts. His concept of the former *(eros)* as a principle of synthesis and unification is on an entirely different plane from that of his libido concept. But in spite of the fact that the theory of life and death instincts was accepted by orthodox analysts, this acceptance did not lead to a fundamental revision of the libido concept, especially as far as clinical work is concerned.

as having an existence of their own. At this point he learns
to give them names. At the same time he learns to handle
them; learns that fire is hot and painful, that mother's body
is warm and pleasureful, that wood is hard and heavy, that
paper is light and can be torn. He learns how to handle
people; that mother will smile when I eat; that she will take
me in her arms when I cry; that she will praise me when I
have a bowel movement. All these experiences become crys-
tallized and integrated in the experience: *I am loved.* I am
loved because I am mother's child. I am loved because I am
helpless. I am loved because I am beautiful, admirable. I am
loved because mother needs me. To put it in a more general
formula: *I am loved for what I am,* or perhaps more accu-
rately, *I am loved because I am.* This experience of being
loved by mother is a passive one. There is nothing I have to
do in order to be loved—mother's love is unconditional. All
I have to do is *to be*—to be her child. Mother's love is bliss,
is peace, it need not be acquired, it need not be deserved.
But there is a negative side, too, to the unconditional quality
of mother's love. Not only does it not need to be deserved—it
also *cannot* be acquired, produced, controlled. If it is there,
it is like a blessing; if it is not there, it is as if all beauty had
gone out of life—and there is nothing I can do to create it.

For most children before the age from eight and a half to
ten,[10] the problem is almost exclusively that of *being loved*—
of being loved for what one is. The child up to this age does
not yet love; he responds gratefully, joyfully to being loved.
At this point of the child's development a new factor enters
into the picture: that of a new feeling of producing love by
one's own activity. For the first time, the child thinks of
giving something to mother (or to father), of producing

[10]Cf. Sullivan's description of this development in *The Interpersonal Theory
of Psychiatry,* W. W. Norton & Co., New York, 1953.

something—a poem, a drawing, or whatever it may be. For the first time in the child's life the idea of love is transformed from being loved into loving; into creating love. It takes many years from this first beginning to the maturing of love. Eventually the child, who may now be an adolescent, has overcome his egocentricity; the other person is not any more primarily a means to the satisfaction of his own needs. The needs of the other person are as important as his own—in fact, they have become more important. To give has become more satisfactory, more joyous, than to receive; to love, more important even than being loved. By loving, he has left the prison cell of aloneness and isolation which was constituted by the state of narcissism and self-centeredness. He feels a sense of new union, of sharing, of oneness. More than that, he feels the potency of producing love by loving—rather than the dependence of receiving by being loved—and for that reason having to be small, helpless, sick—or "good." Infantile love follows the principle: *"I love because I am loved."* Mature love follows the principle: *"I am loved because I love."* Immature love says: *"I love you because I need you."* Mature love says: *"I need you because I love you."*

Closely related to the development of the *capacity* of love is the development of the *object* of love. The first months and years of the child are those where his closest attachment is to the mother. This attachment begins before the moment of birth, when mother and child are still one, although they are two. Birth changes the situation in some respects, but not as much as it would appear. The child, while now living outside of the womb, is still completely dependent on mother. But daily he becomes more independent: he learns to walk, to talk, to explore the world on his own; the relationship to mother loses some of its vital significance, and instead the relationship to father becomes more and more important.

In order to understand this shift from mother to father, we

must consider the essential differences in quality between motherly and fatherly love. We have already spoken about motherly love. Motherly love by its very nature is unconditional. Mother loves the newborn infant because it is her child, not because the child has fulfilled any specific condition, or lived up to any specific expectation. (Of course, when I speak here of mother's and father's love, I speak of the "ideal types"—in Max Weber's sense or of an archetype in Jung's sense—and do not imply that every mother and father loves in that way. I refer to the motherly and fatherly principle, which is represented in the motherly and fatherly person.) Unconditional love corresponds to one of the deepest longings, not only of the child, but of every human being; on the other hand, to be loved because of one's merit, because one deserves it, always leaves doubt; maybe I did not please the person whom I want to love me, maybe this, or that— there is always a fear that love could disappear. Furthermore, "deserved" love easily leaves a bitter feeling that one is not loved for oneself, that one is loved *only* because one pleases, that one is, in the last analysis, not loved at all but used. No wonder that we all cling to the longing for motherly love, as children and also as adults. Most children are lucky enough to receive motherly love (to what extent will be discussed later). As adults the same longing is much more difficult to fulfill. In the most satisfactory development it remains a component of normal erotic love; often it finds expression in religious forms, more often in neurotic forms.

The relationship to father is quite different. Mother is the home we come from, she is nature, soil, the ocean; father does not represent any such natural home. He has little connection with the child in the first years of its life, and his importance for the child in this early period cannot be compared with that of mother. But while father does not represent the natural world, he represents the other pole of human existence; the world of thought, of man-made things, of law and order, of discipline, of travel and adventure. Father is the one who teaches the child, who shows him the road into the world.

Closely related to this function is one which is connected with socio-economic development. When private property came into existence, and when private property could be inherited by one of the sons, father began to look for that son to whom he could leave his property. Naturally, that was the one whom father thought best fitted to become his successor, the son who was most like him, and consequently whom he liked the most. Fatherly love is conditional love. Its principle is "I love you *because* you fulfill my expectations, because you do your duty, because you are like me." In conditional fatherly love we find, as with unconditional motherly love, a negative and a positive aspect. The negative aspect is the very fact that fatherly love has to be deserved, that it can be lost if one does not do what is expected. In the nature of fatherly love lies the fact that obedience becomes the main virtue, that disobedience is the main sin—and its punishment the withdrawal of fatherly love. The positive side is equally important. Since his love is conditioned, I can do something to acquire it, I can work for it; his love is not outside of my control as motherly love is.

The mother's and the father's attitudes toward the child correspond to the child's own needs. The infant needs mother's unconditional love and care physiologically as well as psychically. The child, after six, begins to need father's love, his authority and guidance. Mother has the function of making him secure in life, father has the function of teaching him, guiding him to cope with those problems with which the particular society the child has been born into confronts him. In the ideal case, mother's love does not try to prevent the child from growing up, does not try to put a premium on helplessness. Mother should have faith in life, hence not be overanxious, and thus not infect the child with her anxiety. Part of her life should be the wish that the child become independent and eventually separate from her. Father's love should be guided by principles and expectations; it should be patient and tolerant, rather than threatening and authoritarian. It should give the growing child an increasing sense of competence and eventually permit him to become his own authority and to dispense with that of father.

Eventually, the mature person has come to the point where he is his own mother and his own father. He has, as it were, a motherly and a fatherly conscience. Motherly conscience says: "There is no misdeed, no crime which could deprive you of my love, of my wish for your life and happiness." Fatherly conscience says: "You did wrong, you cannot avoid accepting certain consequences of your wrongdoing, and most of all you must change your ways if I am to like you." The mature person has become free from the outside mother and father figures, and has built them up inside. In contrast to Freud's concept of the super-ego, however, he has built them inside not by *incorporating* mother and father, but by building a motherly conscience on his own capacity for love, and a fatherly conscience on his reason and judgment. Furthermore, the mature person loves with both the motherly and the fatherly conscience, in spite of the fact that they seem to contradict each other. If he would only retain his fatherly conscience, he would become harsh and inhuman. If he would only retain his motherly conscience, he would be apt to lose judgment and to hinder himself and others in their development.

In this development from mother-centered to father-centered attachment, and their eventual synthesis, lies the basis for mental health and the achievement of maturity. In the failure of this development lies the basic cause for neurosis.

While it is beyond the scope of this book to develop this trend of thought more fully, some brief remarks may serve to clarify this statement.

One cause for neurotic development can lie in the fact that a boy has a loving, but overindulgent or domineering mother, and a weak and uninterested father. In this case he may remain fixed at an early mother attachment, and develop into a person who is dependent on mother, feels helpless, has the strivings characteristic of the receptive person, that is, to receive, to be protected, to be taken care of, and who has a lack of fatherly qualities—discipline, independence, an ability to master life by himself. He may try to find "mothers" in everybody, sometimes in women and sometimes in men in a position of authority and power. If, on the other hand, the mother is cold, unresponsive and domineering, he may either transfer the need for motherly protection to his father, and subsequent father figures—in which case the end result is similar to the former case—or he will develop into a onesidedly father-oriented person, completely given to the principles of law, order and authority, and lacking in the ability to expect or to receive unconditional love. This development is further intensified if the father is authoritarian and at the same time strongly attached to the son. What is characteristic of all these neurotic developments is the fact that one principle, the fatherly or the motherly, fails to develop or—and this is the case in the more severe neurotic development—that the roles of mother and father become confused both with regard to persons outside and with regard to these roles within the person. Further examination may show that certain types of neurosis, like obsessional neurosis, develop more on the basis of a one-sided father attachment, while others, like hysteria, alcoholism, inability to assert oneself and to cope with life realistically, and depressions, result from mother-centeredness.

3. The Objects of Love

Love is not primarily a relationship to a specific person; it is an *attitude,* an *orientation* of *character* which determines the relatedness of a person to the world as a whole, not toward one "object" of love. If a person loves only one other person and is indifferent to the rest of his fellow men, his love is not love but a symbiotic attachment, or an enlarged egotism. Yet, most people believe that love is constituted by the object, not by the faculty. In fact, they even believe that it is a proof of the intensity of their love when they do not love anybody except the "loved" person. This is the same fallacy which we have already mentioned above. Because one does not see that love is an activity, a power of the soul, one believes that all that is necessary to find is the right object— and that everything goes by itself afterward. This attitude can be compared to that of a man who wants to paint but who, instead of learning the art, claims that he has just to wait for the right object, and that he will paint beautifully when he finds it. If I truly love one person I love all persons, I love the world, I love life. If I can say to somebody else, "I love you," I must be able to say, "I love in you everybody, I love through you the world, I love in you also myself."

Saying that love is an orientation which refers to all and not to one does not imply, however, the idea that there are no differences between various types of love, which depend on the kind of object which is loved.

Brotherly Love   PHILIA   *[handwritten: care, respect, responsibility + knowledge]*

The most fundamental kind of love, which underlies all types of love, is *brotherly love.* By this I mean the sense of responsibility, care, respect, knowledge of any other human being, the wish to further his life. This is the kind of love the Bible speaks of when it says: love thy neighbor as thyself. Brotherly love is love for all human beings; it is characterized by its very lack of exclusiveness. If I have developed the capacity for love, then I cannot help loving my brothers. In brotherly love there is the experience of union with all men, of human solidarity, of human at-onement. Brotherly love is based on the experience that we all are one. The differences in talents, intelligence, knowledge are negligible in comparison with the identity of the human core common to all men. In order to experience this identity it is necessary to penetrate from the periphery to the core. If I perceive in another person mainly the surface, I perceive mainly the differences, that which separates us. If I penetrate to the core, I perceive our identity, the fact of our brotherhood. This relatedness from center to center—instead of that from periphery to periphery—is "central relatedness." Or as Simone Weil expressed it so beautifully: "The same words [e.g., a man says to his wife, "I love you"] can be commonplace or extraordinary according to the manner in which they are spoken. And this manner depends on the depth of the region in a man's being from which they proceed without the will being able to do anything. And by a marvelous agreement they reach the same region in him who hears them. Thus the hearer can discern, if he has any power of discernment, what is the value of the words."[11]

Brotherly love is love between equals: but, indeed, even as equals we are not always "equal"; inasmuch as we are human, we are all in need of help. Today I, tomorrow you. But this need of help does not mean that the one is helpless,

[11]Simone Weil, *Gravity and Grace*, G. P. Putnam's Sons, New York, 1952, p. 117.

the other powerful. Helplessness is a transitory condition; the ability to stand and walk on one's own feet is the permanent and common one.

Yet, love of the helpless one, love of the poor and the stranger, are the beginning of brotherly love. To love one's flesh and blood is no achievement. The animal loves its young and cares for them. The helpless one loves his master, since his life depends on him; the child loves his parents, since he needs them. Only in the love of those who do not serve a purpose, love begins to unfold. Significantly, in the Old Testament, the central object of man's love is the poor, the stranger, the widow and the orphan, and eventually the national enemy, the Egyptian and the Edomite. By having compassion for the helpless one, man begins to develop love for his brother; and in his love for himself he also loves the one who is in need of help, the frail, insecure human being. Compassion implies the element of knowledge and of identification. "You know the heart of the stranger," says the Old Testament, "for you were strangers in the land of Egypt; . . . *therefore love the stranger!*"[12]

Motherly Love

We have already dealt with the nature of motherly love in a previous section which discussed the difference between motherly and fatherly love. Motherly love, as I said there, is unconditional affirmation of the child's life and his needs. But one important addition to this description must be made here. Affirmation of the child's life has two aspects; one is the care and responsibility absolutely necessary for the preserva-

[12]The same idea has been expressed by Hermann Cohen in his *Religion der Vernunft aus den Quellen des Judentums,* 2nd edition, J. Kaufmann Verlag, Frankfurt am Main, 1929, p. 168 ff.

tion of the child's life and his growth. The other aspect goes
further than mere preservation. It is the attitude which instills in the child a love for living, which gives him the feeling:
it is good to be alive, it is good to be a little boy or girl, it is
good to be on this earth! These two aspects of motherly love
are expressed very succinctly in the Biblical story of creation.
God creates the world, and man. This corresponds to the
simple care and affirmation of existence. But God goes
beyond this minimum requirement. On each day after nature—and man—is created, God says: "It is good." Motherly
love, in this second step, makes the child feel: it is good to
have been born; it instills in the child the *love for life,* and
not only the wish to remain alive. The same idea may be
taken to be expressed in another Biblical symbolism. The
promised land (land is always a mother symbol) is described
as "flowing with milk and honey." Milk is the symbol of the
first aspect of love, that of care and affirmation. Honey sym-
bolizes the sweetness of life, the love for it and the happiness
in being alive. Most mothers are capable of giving "milk," but
only a minority of giving "honey" too. In order to be able to
give honey, a mother must not only be a "good mother," but
a happy person—and this aim is not achieved by many. The
effect on the child can hardly be exaggerated. Mother's love
for life is as infectious as her anxiety is. Both attitudes have
a deep effect on the child's whole personality; one can distin-
guish indeed, among children—and adults—those who got
only "milk" and those who got "milk and honey."

In contrast to brotherly love and erotic love which are love
between equals, the relationship of mother and child is by its
very nature one of inequality, where one needs all the help,
and the other gives it. It is for this altruistic, unselfish character that motherly love has been considered the highest kind
of love, and the most sacred of all emotional bonds. It seems,
however, that the real achievement of motherly love lies not

in the mother's love for the small infant, but in her love for the growing child. Actually, the vast majority of mothers are loving mothers as long as the infant is small and still completely dependent on them. Most women want children, are happy with the new-born child, and eager in their care for it. This is so in spite of the fact that they do not "get" anything in return from the child, except a smile or the expression of satisfaction in his face. It seems that this attitude of love is partly rooted in an instinctive equipment to be found in animals as well as in the human female. But, whatever the weight of this instinctive factor may be, there are also specifically human psychological factors which are responsible for this type of motherly love. One may be found in the narcissistic element in motherly love. Inasmuch as the infant is still felt to be a part of herself, her love and infatuation may be a satisfaction of her narcissism. Another motivation may be found in a mother's wish for power, or possession. The child, being helpless and completely subject to her will, is a natural object of satisfaction for a domineering and possessive woman.

Frequent as these motivations are, they are probably less important and less universal than one which can be called the need for transcendence. This need for transcendence is one of the most basic needs of man, rooted in the fact of his self-awareness, in the fact that he is not satisfied with the role of the creature, that he cannot accept himself as dice thrown out of the cup. He needs to feel as the creator, as one transcending the passive role of being created. There are many ways of achieving this satisfaction of creation; the most natural and also the easiest one to achieve is the mother's care and love for her creation. She transcends herself in the infant, her love for it gives her life meaning and significance. (In the very inability of the male to satisfy his need for transcendence by bearing children lies his urge to transcend himself by the creation of man-made things and of ideas.)

But the child must grow. It must emerge from mother's womb, from mother's breast; it must eventually become a completely separate human being. The very essence of motherly love is to care for the child's growth, and that means to want the child's separation from herself. Here lies the basic difference to erotic love. In erotic love, two people who were separate become one. In motherly love, two people who were one become separate. The mother must not only tolerate, she must wish and support the child's separation. It is only at this stage that motherly love becomes such a difficult task, that it requires unselfishness, the ability to give everything and to want nothing but the happiness of the loved one. It is also at this stage that many mothers fail in their task of motherly love. The narcissistic, the domineering, the possessive woman can succeed in being a "loving" mother as long as the child is small. Only the really loving woman, the woman who is happier in giving than in taking, who is firmly rooted in her own existence, can be a loving mother when the child is in the process of separation.

Motherly love for the growing child, love which wants nothing for oneself, is perhaps the most difficult form of love to be achieved, and all the more deceptive because of the ease with which a mother can love her small infant. But just because of this difficulty, a woman can be a truly loving mother only if she can *love;* if she is able to love her husband, other children, strangers, all human beings. The woman who is not capable of love in this sense can be an affectionate mother as long as the child is small, but she cannot be a loving mother, the test of which is the willingness to bear separation—and even after the separation to go on loving.

Erotic Love (DOES NOT MEAN SEXUALITY)

Brotherly love is love among equals; motherly love is love for the helpless. Different as they are from each other, they have in common that they are by their very nature not restricted to one person. If I love my brother, I love all my brothers; if I love my child, I love all my children; no, beyond that, I love all children, all that are in need of my help. In contrast to both types of love is *erotic love;* it is the craving for complete fusion, for union with one other person. It is by its very nature exclusive and not universal; it is also perhaps the most deceptive form of love there is. ·

First of all, it is often confused with the explosive experience of "falling" in love, the sudden collapse of the barriers which existed until that moment between two strangers. But, as was pointed out before, this experience of sudden intimacy is by its very nature short-lived. After the stranger has become an intimately known person there are no more barriers to be overcome, there is no more sudden closeness to be achieved. The "loved" person becomes as well known as oneself. Or, perhaps I should better say as little known: If there were more depth in the experience of the other person, if one could experience the infiniteness of his personality, the other person would never be so familiar—and the miracle of overcoming the barriers might occur every day anew. But for most people their own person, as well as others, is soon explored and soon exhausted. For them intimacy is established primarily through sexual contact. Since they experience the separateness of the other person primarily as physical separateness, physical union means overcoming separateness.

Beyond that, there are other factors which to many people denote the overcoming of separateness. To speak of one's own personal life, one's hopes and anxieties, to show oneself with one's childlike or childish aspects, to establish a common interest vis-à-vis the world—all this is taken as overcoming separateness. Even to show one's anger, one's hate, one's complete lack of inhibition is taken for intimacy, and this may explain the perverted attraction married couples often have for each other, who seem intimate only when they are in bed or when they give vent to their mutual hate and rage. But all these types of closeness tend to become reduced more and more as time goes on. The consequence is one seeks love with a new person, with a new stranger. Again the stranger is transformed into an "intimate" person, again the experience of falling in love is exhilarating and intense, and again it slowly becomes less and less intense, and ends in the wish for a new conquest, a new love—always with the illusion that the new love will be different from the earlier ones. These illusions are greatly helped by the deceptive character of sexual desire.

Sexual desire aims at fusion—and is by no means only a physical appetite, the relief of a painful tension. But sexual desire can be stimulated by the anxiety of aloneness, by the wish to conquer or be conquered, by vanity, by the wish to hurt and even to destroy, as much as it can be stimulated by love. It seems that sexual desire can easily blend with and be stimulated by any strong emotion, of which love is only one. Because sexual desire is in the minds of most people coupled with the idea of love, they are easily misled to conclude that they love each other when they want each other physically. Love can inspire the wish for sexual union; in this case the physical relationship is lacking in greediness, in a wish to conquer or to be conquered, but is blended with tenderness. If the desire for physical union is not stimulated by love, if erotic love is not also brotherly love, it never leads to union in more than an orgiastic, transitory sense. Sexual attraction creates, for the moment, the illusion of union, yet without love this "union" leaves strangers as far apart as they were before—sometimes it makes them ashamed of each other, or even makes them hate each other, because when the illusion has gone they feel their estrangement even more markedly than before. Tenderness is by no means, as Freud believed, a sublimation of the sexual instinct; it is the direct outcome of brotherly love, and exists in physical as well as in non-physical forms of love.

In erotic love there is an exclusiveness which is lacking in brotherly love and motherly love. This exclusive character of erotic love warrants some further discussion. Frequently the exclusiveness of erotic love is misinterpreted as meaning possessive attachment. One can often find two people "in love" with each other who feel no love for anybody else. Their love is, in fact, an egotism à *deux;* they are two people who identify themselves with each other, and who solve the problem of separateness by enlarging the single individual into two. They have the experience of overcoming aloneness, yet, since they are separated from the rest of mankind, they remain separated from each other and alienated from themselves; their experience of union is an illusion. Erotic love is exclusive, but it loves in the other person all of mankind, all that is alive. It is exclusive only in the sense that I can fuse myself fully and intensely with one person only. Erotic love excludes the love for others only in the sense of erotic fusion, full commitment in all aspects of life—but not in the sense of deep brotherly love.

Erotic love, if it is love, has one premise. That I love from the essence of my being—and experience the other person in the essence of his or her being. In essence, all human beings are identical. We are all part of One; we are One. This being so, it should not make any difference whom we love. Love should be essentially an act of will, of decision to commit my life completely to that of one other person. This is, indeed, the rationale behind the idea of the insolubility of marriage, as it is behind the many forms of traditional marriage in which the two partners never choose each other, but are chosen for each other—and yet are expected to love each other. In contemporary Western culture this idea appears altogether false. Love is supposed to be the outcome of a spontaneous, emotional reaction, of suddenly being gripped by an irresistible feeling. In this view, one sees only the peculiarities of the two individuals involved—and not the fact that all men are part of Adam, and all women part of Eve. One neglects to see an important factor in erotic love, that of *will*. To love somebody is not just a strong feeling—it is a decision, it is a judgment, it is a promise. If love were only a feeling, there would be no basis for the promise to love each other forever. A feeling comes and it may go. How can I judge that it will stay forever, when my act does not involve judgment and decision?

Taking these views into account one may arrive at the position that love is exclusively an act of will and commitment, and that therefore fundamentally it does not matter who the two persons are. Whether the marriage was arranged by others, or the result of individual choice, once the marriage is concluded, the act of will should guarantee the continuation of love. This view seems to neglect the paradoxical character of human nature and of erotic love. We are all One—yet every one of us is a unique, unduplicable entity. In our relationships to others the same paradox is repeated. Inasmuch as we are all one, we can love everybody in the same way in the sense of brotherly love. But inasmuch as we are all also different, erotic love requires certain specific, highly individual elements which exist between some people but not between all.

Both views then, that of erotic love as completely individual attraction, unique between two specific persons, as well as the other view that erotic love is nothing but an act of will, are true—or, as it may be put more aptly, the truth is neither this nor that. Hence the idea of a relationship which can be easily dissolved if one is not successful with it is as erroneous as the idea that under no circumstances must the relationship be dissolved.

Self-Love[13]

While it raises no objection to apply the concept of love to various objects, it is a widespread belief that, while it is virtuous to love others, it is sinful to love oneself. It is assumed that to the degree to which I love myself I do not love others, that self-love is the same as selfishness. This view goes far back in Western thought. Calvin speaks of self-love as "a pest."[14] Freud speaks of self-love in psychiatric terms but, nevertheless, his value judgment is the same as that of Calvin. For him self-love is the same as narcissism, the turning of the libido toward oneself. Narcissism is the earliest stage in human development, and the person who in later life has returned to this narcissistic stage is incapable of love; in the extreme case he is insane. Freud assumes that love is the manifesta-

False BELIEF

[13]Paul Tillich, in a review of *The Sane Society,* in *Pastoral Psychology,* September, 1955, has suggested that it would be better to drop the ambiguous term "self-love" and to replace it with "natural self-affirmation" or "paradoxical self-acceptance." Much as I can see the merits of this suggestion, I cannot agree with him in this point. In the term "self-love" the paradoxical element in self-love is contained more clearly. The fact is expressed that love is an attitude which is the same toward all objects, including myself. It must also not be forgotten that the term "self-love," in the sense in which it is used here, has a history. The Bible speaks of self-love when it commands to "love thy neighbor *as thyself,*" and Meister Eckhart speaks of self-love in the very same sense.

[14]John Calvin, *Institutes of the Christian Religion,* translated by J. Albau, Presbyterian Board of Christian Education, Philadelphia, 1928, Chap. 7, par. 4, p. 622.

tion of libido, and that the libido is either turned toward others—love; or toward oneself—self-love. Love and self-love are thus mutually exclusive in the sense that the more there is of one, the less there is of the other. If self-love is bad, it follows that unselfishness is virtuous.

These questions arise: Does psychological observation support the thesis that there is a basic contradiction between love for oneself and love for others? Is love for oneself the same phenomenon as selfishness, or are they opposites? Furthermore, is the selfishness of modern man really a *concern for himself* as an individual, with all his intellectual, emotional and sensual potentialities? Has "he" not become an appendage of his socio-economic role? *Is his selfishness identical with self-love or is it not caused by the very lack of it?*

Before we start the discussion of the psychological aspect of selfishness and self-love, the logical fallacy in the notion that love for others and love for oneself are mutually exclusive should be stressed. If it is a virtue to love my neighbor as a human being, it must be a virtue—and not a vice—to love myself, since I am a human being too. There is no concept of man in which I myself am not included. A doctrine which proclaims such an exclusion proves itself to be intrinsically contradictory. The idea expressed in the Biblical "Love thy neighbor as thyself!" implies that respect for one's own integrity and uniqueness, love for and understanding of one's own self, cannot be separated from respect and love and understanding for another individual. The love for my own self is inseparably connected with the love for any other being.

We have come now to the basic psychological premises on which the conclusions of our argument are built. Generally, these premises are as follows: not only others, but we ourselves are the "object" of our feelings and attitudes; the attitudes toward others and toward ourselves, far from being contradictory, are basically *conjunctive*. With regard to the problem under discussion this means: love of others and love of ourselves are not alternatives. On the contrary, an attitude of love toward themselves will be found in all those who are capable of loving others. *Love, in principle, is indivisible as far as the connection between "objects" and one's own self is concerned.* Genuine love is an expression of productiveness and implies care, respect, responsibility and knowledge. It is not an "affect" in the sense of being affected by somebody, but an active striving for the growth and happiness of the loved person, rooted in one's own capacity to love.

To love somebody is the actualization and concentration of the power to love. The basic affirmation contained in love is directed toward the beloved person as an incarnation of essentially human qualities. Love of one person implies love of man as such. The kind of "division of labor," as William James calls it, by which one loves one's family but is without feeling for the "stranger," is a sign of a basic inability to love. Love of man is not, as is frequently supposed, an abstraction coming after the love for a specific person, but it is its premise, although genetically it is acquired in loving specific individuals.

From this it follows that my own self must be as much an object of my love as another person. *The affirmation of one's own life, happiness, growth, freedom is rooted in one's capacity to love,* i.e., in care, respect, responsibility, and knowledge. If an individual is able to love productively, he loves himself too; if he can love *only* others, he cannot love at all.

Granted that love for oneself and for others in principle is conjunctive, how do we explain selfishness, which obviously excludes any genuine concern for others? The *selfish* person is interested only in himself, wants everything for himself, feels no pleasure in giving, but only in taking. The world outside is looked at only from the standpoint of what he can get out of it; he lacks interest in the needs of others, and respect for their dignity and integrity. He can see nothing but himself; he judges everyone and everything from its usefulness to him; he is basically unable to love. Does not this prove that concern for others and concern for oneself are unavoidable alternatives? This would be so if selfishness and self-love were identical. But that assumption is the very fallacy which has led to so many mistaken conclusions concerning our problem. *Selfishness and self-love, far from being identical, are actually opposites.* The selfish person does not love himself too much but too little; in fact he hates himself. This lack of fondness and care for himself, which is only one expression of his lack of productiveness, leaves him empty and frustrated. He is necessarily unhappy and anxiously concerned to snatch from life the satisfactions which he blocks himself from attaining. He seems to care too much for himself, but actually he only makes an unsuccessful attempt to cover up and compensate for his failure to care for his real self. Freud holds that the selfish person is narcissistic, as if he had withdrawn his love from others and turned it toward his own person. *It is true that selfish persons are incapable of loving others, but they are not capable of loving themselves either.*

It is easier to understand selfishness by comparing it with greedy concern for others, as we find it, for instance, in an oversolicitous mother. While she consciously believes that she is particularly fond of her child, she has actually a deeply repressed hostility toward the object of her concern. She is overconcerned not because she loves the child too much, but because she has to compensate for her lack of capacity to love him at all.

This theory of the nature of selfishness is borne out by psychoanalytic experience with neurotic "unselfishness," a symptom of neurosis observed in not a few people who usu-

ally are troubled not by this symptom but by others connected with it, like depression, tiredness, inability to work,
failure in love relationships, and so on. Not only is unselfishness not felt as a "symptom"; it is often the one redeeming
character trait on which such people pride themselves. The
"unselfish" person "does not want anything for himself"; he
"lives only for others," is proud that he does not consider
himself important. He is puzzled to find that in spite of his
unselfishness he is unhappy, and that his relationships to
those closest to him are unsatisfactory. Analytic work shows
that his unselfishness is not something apart from his other
symptoms but one of them, in fact often the most important
one; that he is paralyzed in his capacity to love or to enjoy
anything; that he is pervaded by hostility toward life and that
behind the façade of unselfishness a subtle but not less intense self-centeredness is hidden. This person can be cured
only if his unselfishness too is interpreted as a symptom along
with the others, so that his lack of productiveness, which is
at the root of both his unselfishness *and* his other troubles,
can be corrected.

The nature of unselfishness becomes particularly apparent
in its effect on others, and most frequently in our culture in
the effect the "unselfish" mother has on her children. She
believes that by her unselfishness her children will experience what it means to be loved and to learn, in turn, what
it means to love. The effect of her unselfishness, however,
does not at all correspond to her expectations. The children
do not show the happiness of persons who are convinced that
they are loved; they are anxious, tense, afraid of the mother's
disapproval and anxious to live up to her expectations. Usually, they are affected by their mother's hidden hostility toward life, which they sense rather than recognize clearly,
and eventually they become imbued with it themselves. Altogether, the effect of the "unselfish" mother is not too dif-

ferent from that of the selfish one; indeed, it is often worse, because the mother's unselfishness prevents the children from criticizing her. They are put under the obligation not to disappoint her; they are taught, under the mask of virtue, dislike for life. If one has a chance to study the effect of a mother with genuine self-love, one can see that there is nothing more conducive to giving a child the experience of what love, joy and happiness are than being loved by a mother who loves herself.

These ideas on self-love cannot be summarized better than by quoting Meister Eckhart on this topic: "If you love yourself, you love everybody else as you do yourself. As long as you love another person less than you love yourself, you will not really succeed in loving yourself, but if you love all alike, including yourself, you will love them as one person and that person is both God and man. Thus he is a great and righteous person who, loving himself, loves all others equally."[15]

Love of God

It has been stated above that the basis for our need to love lies in the experience of separateness and the resulting need to overcome the anxiety of separateness by the experience of union. The religious form of love, that which is called the love of God, is, psychologically speaking, not different. It springs from the need to overcome separateness and to achieve union. In fact, the love of God has as many different qualities and aspects as the love of man has—and to a large extent we find the same differences.

In all theistic religions, whether they are polytheistic or monotheistic, God stands for the highest value, the most

[15] *Meister Eckhart*, translated by R. B. Blakney, Harper & Brothers, New York, 1941, p. 204.

desirable good. Hence, the specific meaning of God depends on what is the most desirable good for a person. The understanding of the concept of God must, therefore, start with an analysis of the character structure of the person who worships God.

The development of the human race as far as we have any knowledge of it can be characterized as the emergence of man from nature, from mother, from the bonds of blood and soil. In the beginning of human history man, though thrown out of the original unity with nature, still clings to these primary bonds. He finds his security by going back, or holding on to these primary bonds. He still feels identified with the world of animals and trees, and tries to find unity by remaining one with the natural world. Many primitive religions bear witness to this stage of development. An animal is transformed into a totem; one wears animal masks in the most solemn religious acts, or in war; one worships an animal as God. At a later stage of development, when human skill has developed to the point of artisan and artistic skill, when man is not dependent any more exclusively on the gifts of nature—the fruit he finds and the animal he kills—man transforms the product of his own hand into a god. This is the stage of the worship of idols made of clay, silver or gold. Man projects his own powers and skills into the things he makes, and thus in an alienated fashion worships his prowess, his possessions. At a still later stage man gives his gods the form of human beings. It seems that this can happen only when he has become still more aware of himself, and when he has discovered man as the highest and most dignified "thing" in the world. In this phase of anthropomorphic god worship we find a development in two dimensions. The one refers to the female or male nature of the gods, the other to the degree of maturity which man has achieved, and which determines the nature of his gods and the nature of his love of them.

Let us first speak of the development from mother-centered to father-centered religions. According to the great and decisive discoveries of Bachofen and Morgan in the middle of the nineteenth century, and in spite of the rejection their findings have found in most academic circles, there can be little doubt that there was a matriarchal phase of religion preceding the patriarchal one, at least in many cultures. In the matriarchal phase, the highest being is the mother. She is the goddess, she is also the authority in family and society. In order to understand the essence of matriarchal religion, we have only to remember what has been said about the essence of motherly love. Mother's love is unconditional, it is all-protective, all-enveloping; because it is unconditional it can also not be controlled or acquired. Its presence gives the loved person a sense of bliss; its absence produces a sense of lostness and utter despair. Since mother loves her children because they are her children, and not because they are "good," obedient, or fulfill her wishes and commands, mother's love is based on equality. All men are equal, because they all are children of a mother, because they all are children of Mother Earth.

The next stage of human evolution, the only one of which we have thorough knowledge and do not need to rely on inferences and reconstruction, is the patriarchal phase. In this phase the mother is dethroned from her supreme position, and the father becomes the Supreme Being, in religion as well as in society. The nature of fatherly love is that he makes demands, establishes principles and laws, and that his love for the son depends on the obedience of the latter to these demands. He likes best the son who is most like him, who is most obedient and who is best fitted to become his successor, as the inheritor of his possessions. (The development of patriarchal society goes together with the development of private property.) As a consequence, patriarchal society is hierarchical; the equality of the brothers gives way to competition and mutual strife. Whether we think of the Indian, Egyptian or Greek cultures, or of the Jewish-Christian, or Islamic religions, we are in the middle of a patriarchal world, with its male gods, over whom one chief god reigns, or where all gods have been eliminated with the exception of the One, *the* God. However, since the wish for mother's love cannot be eradicated from the hearts of man, it is not surprising that the figure of the loving mother could never be fully driven out from the pantheon. In the Jewish religion, the mother aspects of God are reintroduced especially in the various currents of mysticism. In the Catholic religion, Mother is symbolized by the Church, and by the Virgin. Even in Protestantism, the figure of Mother has not been entirely eradicated, although she remains hidden. Luther established as his main principle that nothing that man *does* can procure God's love. God's love is Grace, the religious attitude is to have faith in this grace, and to make oneself small and helpless; no good works can influence God—or make God love us, as Catholic doctrines postulated. We can recognize here that the Catholic doctrine of good works is part of the patriarchal picture; I can procure father's love by obedience and by fulfilling his demands. The Lutheran doctrine, on the other hand, in spite of its manifest patriarchal character carries within it a hidden matriarchal element. Mother's love cannot be acquired; it is there, or it is not there; all I can do is to have faith (as the Psalmist says, "Thou hadst let me have faith into my mother's breasts."[16]) and to transform myself into the helpless, powerless child. But it is the peculiarity of Luther's faith that the figure of the mother has been eliminated from the manifest picture, and replaced by that of the father; instead of the certainty of being loved by

[16]Psalm 22:9.

mother, intense doubt, hoping against hope for unconditional love by *father*, has become the paramount feature.

I had to discuss this difference between the matriarchal
and the patriarchal elements in religion in order to show that
the character of the love of God depends on the respective
weight of the matriarchal and the patriarchal aspects of religion. The patriarchal aspect makes me love God like a father;
I assume he is just and strict, that he punishes and rewards;
and eventually that he will elect me as his favorite son; as
God elected Abraham-Israel, as Isaac elected Jacob, as God
elects his favorite nation. In the matriarchal aspect of religion, I love God as an all-embracing mother. I have faith in
her love, that no matter whether I am poor and powerless,
no matter whether I have sinned, she will love me, she will
not prefer any other of her children to me; whatever happens to me, she will rescue me, will save me, will forgive me.
Needless to say, my love for God and God's love for me
cannot be separated. If God is a father, he loves me like a son
and I love him like a father. If God is mother, her and my love
are determined by this fact.

This difference between the motherly and the fatherly
aspects of the love of God is, however, only one factor in
determining the nature of this love; the other factor is the
degree of maturity reached by the individual, hence in his
concept of God and in his love for God.

Since the evolution of the human race shifted from a
mother-centered to a father-centered structure of society, as
well as of religion, we can trace the development of a maturing love mainly in the development of patriarchal religion.[17]

[17]This holds true especially for the monotheistic religions of the West. In
Indian religions the mother figures retained a good deal of influence, for
instance in the Goddess Kali; in Buddhism and Taoism the concept of a
God—or a Goddess—was without essential significance, if not altogether
eliminated.

In the beginning of this development we find a despotic, jealous God, who considers man, whom he created, as his property, and is entitled to do with him whatever he pleases. This is the phase of religion in which God drives man out of paradise, lest he eat from the tree of knowledge and thus could become God himself; this is the phase in which God decides to destroy the human race by the flood, because none of them pleases him, with the exception of the favorite son, Noah; this is the phase in which God demands from Abraham that he kill his only, his beloved son, Isaac, to prove his love for God by the act of ultimate obedience. But simultaneously a new phase begins; God makes a covenant with Noah, in which he promises never to destroy the human race again, a covenant by which he is bound himself. Not only is he bound by his promises, he is also bound by his own principle, that of justice, and on this basis God must yield to Abraham's demand to spare Sodom if there are at least ten just men. But the development goes further than transforming God from the figure of a despotic tribal chief into a loving father, into a father who himself is bound by the principles which he has postulated; it goes in the direction of transforming God from the figure of a father into a symbol of his principles, those of justice, truth and love. God *is* truth, God *is* justice. In this development God ceases to be a person, a man, a father; he becomes the symbol of the principle of unity behind the manifoldness of phenomena, of the vision of the flower which will grow from the spiritual seed within man. God cannot have a name. A name always denotes a thing, or a person, something finite. How can God have a name, if he is not a person, not a thing?

The most striking incident of this change lies in the Biblical story of God's revelation to Moses. When Moses tells him that the Hebrews will not believe that God has sent him, unless he can tell them God's name (how could idol worshipers comprehend a nameless God, since the very essence of an idol is to have a name?), God makes a concession. He tells Moses that his name is "I am becoming that which I am becoming." "I-am-becoming is my name." The "I-am-becoming" means that God is not finite, not a person, not a "being." The most adequate translation of the sentence would be: tell them that "my name is nameless." The prohibition to make any image of God, to pronounce his name in vain, eventually to pronounce his name at all, aims at the same goal, that of freeing man from the idea that God is a father, that he is a person. In the subsequent theological development, the idea is carried further in the principle that one must not even give God any positive attribute. To say of God that he is wise, strong, good implies again that he is a person; the most I can do is to say what God is *not*, to state negative attributes, to postulate that he is *not* limited, not unkind, not unjust. The more I know what God is *not*, the more knowledge I have of God.[18]

Following the maturing idea of monotheism in its further consequences can lead only to one conclusion: not to mention God's name at all, not to speak *about* God. Then God becomes what he potentially is in monotheistic theology, the nameless One, an inexpressible stammer, referring to the unity underlying the phenomenal universe, the ground of all existence; God becomes truth, love, justice. God is I, inasmuch as I am human.

Quite evidently this evolution from the anthropomorphic to the pure monotheistic principle makes all the difference to the nature of the love of God. The God of Abraham can be loved, or feared, as a father, sometimes his forgiveness, sometimes his anger being the dominant aspect. Inasmuch as

[18]Cf. Maimonides' concept of the negative attributes in *The Guide for the Perplexed*.

God is the father, I am the child. I have not emerged fully from the autistic wish for omniscience and omnipotence. I have not yet acquired the objectivity to realize my limitations as a human being, my ignorance, my helplessness. I still claim, like a child, that there must be a father who rescues me, who watches me, who punishes me, a father who likes me when I am obedient, who is flattered by my praise and angry because of my disobedience. Quite obviously, the majority of people have, in their personal development, not overcome this infantile stage, and hence the belief in God to most people is the belief in a helping father—a childish illusion. In spite of the fact that this concept of religion has been overcome by some of the great teachers of the human race, and by a minority of men, it is still the dominant form of religion.

Inasmuch as this is so, the criticism of the idea of God, as it was expressed by Freud, is quite correct. The error, however, was in the fact that he ignored the other aspect of monotheistic religion, and its true kernel, the logic of which leads exactly to the negation of this concept of God. The truly religious person, if he follows the essence of the monotheistic idea, does not pray for anything, does not expect anything from God; he does not love God as a child loves his father or his mother; he has acquired the humility of sensing his limitations, to the degree of knowing that he knows nothing about God. God becomes to him a symbol in which man, at an earlier stage of his evolution, has expressed the totality of that which man is striving for, the realm of the spiritual world, of love, truth and justice. He has faith in the principles which "God" represents; he thinks truth, lives love and justice, and considers all of his life only valuable inasmuch as it gives him the chance to arrive at an ever fuller unfolding of his human powers—as the only reality that matters, as the only object of "ultimate concern"; and, eventually, he does not speak about God—nor even mention his name. To love God, if he were going to use this word, would mean, then, to long for the attainment of the full capacity to love, for the realization of that which "God" stands for in oneself.

From this point of view, the logical consequence of monotheistic thought is the negation of all "theo-logy," of all "knowledge about God." Yet, there remains a difference between such a radical non-theological view and a non-theistic system, as we find it, for instance, in early Buddhism or in Taoism.

In all theistic systems, even a non-theological, mystical one, there is the assumption of the reality of the spiritual realm, as one transcending man, giving meaning and validity to man's spiritual powers and his striving for salvation and inner birth. In a non-theistic system, there exists no spiritual realm outside of man or transcending him. The realm of love, reason and justice exists as a reality only because, and inasmuch as, man has been able to develop these powers in himself throughout the process of his evolution. In this view there is no meaning to life, except the meaning man himself gives to it; man is utterly alone except inasmuch as he helps another.

Having spoken of the love of God, I want to make it clear that I myself do not think in terms of a theistic concept, and that to me the concept of God is only a historically conditioned one, in which man has expressed his experience of his higher powers, his longing for truth and for unity at a given historical period. But I believe also that the consequences of strict monotheism and a non-theistic ultimate concern with the spiritual reality are two views which, though different, need not fight each other.

At this point, however, another dimension of the problem of the love of God arises, which must be discussed in order to fathom the complexity of the problem. I refer to a fundamental difference in the religious attitude between the East

(China and India) and the West; this difference can be expressed in terms of logical concepts. Since Aristotle, the Western world has followed the logical principles of Aristotelian philosophy. This logic is based on the law of identity which states that A is A, the law of contradiction (A is not non-A) and the law of the excluded middle (A cannot be A *and* non-A, neither A *nor* non-A). Aristotle explains his position very clearly in the following sentence: "It is impossible for the same thing at the same time to belong and not to belong to the same thing and in the same respect; and whatever other distinctions we might add to meet dialectical objections, let them be added. This, then, is the most certain of all principles. . . ."[19]

This axiom of Aristotelian logic has so deeply imbued our habits of thought that it is felt to be "natural" and self-evident, while on the other hand the statement that X is A *and* not A seems to be nonsensical. (Of course, the statement refers to the subject X at a given time, not to X now and X later, or one aspect of X as against another aspect.)

In opposition to Aristotelian logic is what one might call *paradoxical logic,* which assumes that A and non-A do not exclude each other as predicates of X. Paradoxical logic was predominant in Chinese and Indian thinking, in the philosophy of Heraclitus, and then again, under the name of dialectics, it became the philosophy of Hegel, and of Marx. The general principle of paradoxical logic has been clearly described by Lao-tse. *"Words that are strictly true seem to be paradoxical."*[20] And by Chuang-tzu: "That which is one is

[19]Aristotle, *Metaphysics,* Book Gamma, 1005b. 20. Quoted from *Aristotle's Metaphysics,* newly translated by Richard Hope, Columbia University Press, New York, 1952.

[20]Lao-tse, *The Tâo Teh King, The Sacred Books of the East,* ed. by F. Max Mueller, Vol. XXXIX, Oxford University Press, London, 1927, p. 120

one. That which is not-one, is also one." These formulations of paradoxical logic are positive: *it is and it is not.* Another formulation is negative: *it is neither this nor that.* The former expression of thought we find in Taoistic thought, in Heraclitus and again in Hegelian dialectics; the latter formulation is frequent in Indian philosophy.

Although it would transcend the scope of this book to give a more detailed description of the difference between Aristotelian and paradoxical logic, I shall mention a few illustrations in order to make the principle more understandable. Paradoxical logic in Western thought has its earliest philosophical expression in Heraclitus' philosophy. He assumes the conflict between opposites is the basis of all existence. "They do not understand," he says, "that the all-One, conflicting in itself, is identical with itself: *conflicting harmony* as in the bow and in the lyre."[21] Or still more clearly: "We go into the same river, and yet not in the same; *it is we and it is not we.*"[22] Or "One and the same manifests itself in things as living and dead, waking and sleeping, young and old."[23]

In Lao-tse's philosophy the same idea is expressed in a more poetic form. A characteristic example of Taoist paradoxical thinking is the following statement: "Gravity is the root of lightness; stillness the ruler of movement."[24] Or "The Tâo in its regular course does nothing and so there is nothing which he does not do."[25] Or "My words are very easy to know, and very easy to practice; but there is no one in the

[21]W. Capelle, *Die Vorsokratiker,* Alfred Kroener Verlag, Stuttgart, 1953, p. 134. (My translation. E. F.)

[22]*Ibid.,* p. 132.

[23]*Ibid.,* p. 133.

[24]Mueller, *op. cit.,* p. 69.

[25]*Ibid.,* p. 79.

world who is able to know and able to practice them."[26] In Taoist thinking, just as in Indian and Socratic thinking, the highest step to which thought can lead is to know that we do not know. "To know and yet [think] we do not know is the highest [attainment]; not to know [and yet think] we do know is a disease."[27] It is only a consequence of this philosophy that the highest God cannot be named. The ultimate reality, the ultimate One cannot be caught in words or in thoughts. As Lao-tse puts it, "The Tâo that can be trodden is not the enduring and unchanging Tâo. The name that can be named is not the enduring and unchanging name."[28] Or, in a different formulation, "We look at it, and we do not see it, and we name it the 'Equable.' We listen to it, and we do not hear it, and we name it the 'Inaudible.' We try to grasp it, and do not get hold of it, and we name it the 'Subtle.' With these three qualities, it can not be made the subject of description; and hence we blend them together and obtain The One."[29] And still another formulation of the same idea: "He who knows [the Tâo] does not [care to] speak [about it]; he who is [however ready to] speak about it does not know it."[30]

Brahmanic philosophy was concerned with the relationship between manifoldness (of phenomena) and unity (Brahman). But paradoxical philosophy is neither in India nor in China to be confused with a *dualistic* standpoint. The harmony (unity) consists in the conflicting position from which it is made up. "Brahmanical thinking was centered from the beginning around the paradox of the simultaneous antago-

[26]*Ibid.*, p. 112.

[27]*Ibid.*, p. 113.

[28]*Ibid.*, p. 47.

[29]*Ibid.*, p. 57.

[30]*Ibid.*, p. 100.

nisms—yet—identity of the manifest forces and forms of the phenomenal world. . . ."[31] The ultimate power in the Universe as well as in man transcends both the conceptual and the sensual sphere. It is therefore "neither this nor thus." But, as Zimmer remarks, "there is no antagonism between 'real and unreal' in this strictly non-dualistic realization."[32] In their search for unity behind manifoldness, the Brahman thinkers came to the conclusion that the perceived pair of opposites reflects the nature not of things but of the perceiving mind. The perceiving thought must transcend itself if it is to attain true reality. Opposition is a category of man's mind, not in itself an element of reality. In the Rig-Veda the principle is expressed in this form: "I am the two, the life force and the life material, the two at once." The ultimate consequence of the idea that thought can only perceive in contradictions has found an even more drastic sequence in Vedantic thinking, which postulates that thought—with all its fine distinction—was "only a more subtle horizon of ignorance, in fact the most subtle of all the deluding devices of maya."[33]

Paradoxical logic has a significant bearing on the concept of God. Inasmuch as God represents the ultimate reality, and inasmuch as the human mind perceives reality in contradictions, no positive statement can be made of God. In the Vedantas the idea of an omniscient and omnipotent God is considered the ultimate form of ignorance.[34] We see here the connection with the namelessness of the Tao, the nameless name of the God who reveals himself to Moses, of the "abso-

[31]H. R. Zimmer, *Philosophies of India,* Pantheon Books, New York, 1951.

[32]*Ibid.,*

[33]*Ibid.,* p. 424.

[34]Cf. Zimmer, *ibid.,* p. 424.

lute Nothing" of Meister Eckhart. Man can only know the negation, never the position of ultimate reality. "Meanwhile man can not know what God is, even though he be ever so well aware of what God is not. . . . Thus contented with nothing, the mind clamors for the highest good of all."[35] For Meister Eckhart, "The Divine One is a negation of negations, and a denial of denials. . . . Every creature contains a negation: one denies that it is the other."[36] It is only a further consequence that God becomes for Meister Eckhart "The absolute Nothing," just as the ultimate reality is the "En Sof," the Endless One, for the Kabalah.

I have discussed the difference between Aristotelian and paradoxical logic in order to prepare the ground for an important difference in the concept of the love of God. The teachers of paradoxical logic say that man can perceive reality only in contradictions, and can never perceive in *thought* the ultimate reality-unity, the One itself. This led to the consequence that one did not seek as the ultimate aim to find the answer in *thought.* Thought can only lead us to the knowledge that it cannot give us the ultimate answer. The world of thought remains caught in the paradox. The only way in which the world can be grasped ultimately lies, not in thought, but in the act, in the experience of oneness. Thus paradoxical logic leads to the conclusion that the love of God is neither the knowledge of God in thought, nor the thought of one's love of God, but the act of experiencing the oneness with God.

This leads to the emphasis on the right way of living. All of life, every little and every important action, is devoted to the knowledge of God, but a knowledge not in right thought,

[35]*Meister Eckhart,* translated by R. B. Blakney, Harper & Brothers, New York, 1941, p. 114.

[36]*Ibid.,* p. 247. Cf. also the negative theology of Maimonides.

but in right action. This can be clearly seen in Oriental religions. In Brahmanism as well as in Buddhism and Taoism, the ultimate aim of religion is not the right belief, but the right action. We find the same emphasis in the Jewish religion. There was hardly ever a schism over belief in the Jewish tradition (the one great exception, the difference between Pharisees and Sadducees, was essentially one of two opposite social classes). The emphasis of the Jewish religion was (especially from the beginning of our era on) on the right way of living, the Halacha (this word actually having the same meaning as the Tao).

In modern history, the same principle is expressed in the thought of Spinoza, Marx and Freud. In Spinoza's philosophy the emphasis is shifted from the right belief to the right conduct of life. Marx stated the same principle when he said, "The philosophers have interpreted the world in different ways—the task is to transform it." Freud's paradoxical logic leads him to the process of psychoanalytic therapy, the ever deepening experience of oneself.

From the standpoint of paradoxical logic the emphasis is not on thought, but on the act. This attitude had several other consequences. First of all, it led to the *tolerance* which we find in Indian and Chinese religious development. If the right thought is not the ultimate truth, and not the way to salvation, there is no reason to fight others, whose thinking has arrived at different formulations. This tolerance is beautifully expressed in the story of several men who were asked to describe an elephant in the dark. One, touching his trunk, said "this animal is like a water pipe"; another, touching his ear, said "this animal is like a fan"; a third, touching his legs, described the animal as a pillar.

Secondly, the paradoxical standpoint led to the emphasis on *transforming man*, rather than to the development of *dogma* on the one hand, and *science* on the other. From the

Indian, Chinese and mystical standpoints, the religious task of man is not to think right, but to act right, and/or to become one with the One in the act of concentrated meditation.

The opposite is true for the main stream of Western thought. Since one expected to find the ultimate truth in the right thought, major emphasis was on thought, although right action was held to be important too. In religious development this led to the formulation of dogmas, endless arguments about dogmatic formulations, and intolerance of the "non-believer" or heretic. It furthermore led to the emphasis on "believing in God" as the main aim of a religious attitude. This, of course, did not mean that there was not also the concept that one ought to live right. But nevertheless, the person who believed in God—even if he did not *live* God— felt himself to be superior to the one who lived God, but did not "believe" in him.

The emphasis on thought has also another and historically a very important consequence. The idea that one could find the truth in thought led not only to dogma, but also to science. In scientific thought, the correct thought is all that matters, both from the aspect of intellectual honesty, as well as from the aspect of the application of scientific thought to practice—that is, to technique.

In short, paradoxical thought led to tolerance and an effort toward self-transformation. The Aristotelian standpoint led to dogma and science, to the Catholic Church, and to the discovery of atomic energy.

The consequences of this difference between the two standpoints for the problem of the love of God have already been explained implicitly, and need only to be summarized briefly.

In the dominant Western religious system, the love of God is essentially the same as the belief in God, in God's existence,

God's justice, God's love. The love of God is essentially a thought experience. In the Eastern religions and in mysticism, the love of God is an intense feeling experience of oneness, inseparably linked with the expression of this love in every act of living. The most radical formulation has been given to this goal by Meister Eckhart: "If therefore I am changed into God and He makes me one with Himself, then, by the living God, there is no distinction between us. . . . Some people imagine that they are going to see God, that they are going to see God as if he were standing yonder, and they here, but it is not to be so. God and I: we are one. By knowing God I take him to myself. By loving God, I penetrate him."[37]

We can return now to an important parallel between the love for one's parents and the love for God. The child starts out by being attached to his mother as "the ground of all being." He feels helpless and needs the all-enveloping love of mother. He then turns to father as the new center of his affections, father being a guiding principle for thought and action; in this stage he is motivated by the need to acquire father's praise, and to avoid his displeasure. In the stage of full maturity he has freed himself from the person of mother and of father as protecting and commanding powers; he has established the motherly and fatherly principles in himself. He has become his own father and mother; he *is* father and mother. In the history of the human race we see—and can anticipate—the same development: from the beginning of the love for God as the helpless attachment to a mother Goddess, through the obedient attachment to a fatherly God, to a mature stage where God ceases to be an outside power, where man has incorporated the principles of love and justice into himself, where he has become one with God, and

[37] *Meister Eckhart, op. cit.,* pp. 181–2.

eventually, to a point where he speaks of God only in a poetic, symbolic sense.

From these considerations it follows that the love for God cannot be separated from the love for one's parents. If a person does not emerge from incestuous attachment to mother, clan, nation, if he retains the childish dependence on a punishing and rewarding father, or any other authority, he cannot develop a more mature love for God; then his religion is that of the earlier phase of religion, in which God was experienced as an all-protective mother or a punishing-rewarding father.

In contemporary religion we find all the phases, from the earliest and most primitive development to the highest, still present. The word "God" denotes the tribal chief as well as the "absolute Nothing." In the same way, each individual retains in himself, in his unconscious, as Freud has shown, all the stages from the helpless infant on. The question is to what point he has grown. One thing is certain: the nature of his love for God corresponds to the nature of his love for man, and furthermore, the real quality of his love for God and man often is unconscious—covered up and rationalized by a more mature *thought* of what his love is. Love for man, furthermore, while directly embedded in his relations to his family, is in the last analysis determined by the structure of the society in which he lives. If the social structure is one of submission to authority—overt authority or the anonymous authority of the market and public opinion—his concept of God must be infantile and far from the mature concept, the seeds of which are to be found in the history of monotheistic religion.

III

LOVE AND ITS DISINTEGRATION IN CONTEMPORARY WESTERN SOCIETY

If love is a capacity of the mature, productive character, it follows that the capacity to love in an individual living in any given culture depends on the influence this culture has on the character of the average person. If we speak about love in contemporary Western culture, we mean to ask whether the social structure of Western civilization and the spirit resulting from it are conducive to the development of love. To raise the question is to answer it in the negative. No objective observer of our Western life can doubt that love—brotherly love, motherly love, and erotic love—is a relatively rare phenomenon, and that its place is taken by a number of forms of pseudo-love which are in reality so many forms of the disintegration of love.

Capitalistic society is based on the principle of political freedom on the one hand, and of the market as the regulator of all economic, hence social relations, on the other. The commodity market determines the conditions under which

75

commodities are exchanged, the labor market regulates the acquisition and sale of labor. Both useful things and useful human energy and skill are transformed into commodities which are exchanged without the use of force and without fraud under the conditions of the market. Shoes, useful and needed as they may be, have no economic value (exchange value) if there is no demand for them on the market; human energy and skill are without exchange value if there is no demand for them under existing market conditions. The owner of capital can buy labor and command it to work for the profitable investment of his capital. The owner of labor must sell it to capitalists under the existing market conditions, unless he is to starve. This economic structure is reflected in a hierarchy of values. Capital commands labor; amassed things, that which is dead, are of superior value to labor, to human powers, to that which is alive.

This has been the basic structure of capitalism since its beginning. But while it is still characteristic of modern capitalism, a number of factors have changed which give contemporary capitalism its specific qualities and which have a profound influence on the character structure of modern man. As the result of the development of capitalism we witness an ever-increasing process of centralization and concentration of capital. The large enterprises grow in size continuously, the smaller ones are squeezed out. The ownership of capital invested in these enterprises is more and more separated from the function of managing them. Hundreds of thousands of stockholders "own" the enterprise; a managerial bureaucracy which is well paid, but which does not own the enterprise, manages it. This bureaucracy is less interested in making maximum profits than in the expansion of the enterprise, and in their own power. The increasing concentration of capital and the emergence of a powerful managerial bureaucracy are paralleled by the development of the labor movement. Through the unionization of labor, the individual worker does not have to bargain on the labor market by and for himself; he is united in big labor unions, also led by a powerful bureaucracy which represents him vis-à-vis the industrial colossi. The initiative has been shifted, for better or worse, in the fields of capital as well as in those of labor, from the individual to the bureaucracy. An increasing number of people cease to be independent, and become dependent on the managers of the great economic empires.

Another decisive feature resulting from this concentration of capital, and characteristic of modern capitalism, lies in the specific way of the organization of work. Vastly centralized enterprises with a radical division of labor lead to an organization of work where the individual loses his individuality, where he becomes an expendable cog in the machine. The human problem of modern capitalism can be formulated in this way:

Modern capitalism needs men who co-operate smoothly and in large numbers; who want to consume more and more; and whose tastes are standardized and can be easily influenced and anticipated. It needs men who feel free and independent, not subject to any authority or principle or conscience—yet willing to be commanded, to do what is expected of them, to fit into the social machine without friction; who can be guided without force, led without leaders, prompted without aim—except the one to make good, to be on the move, to function, to go ahead.

What is the outcome? Modern man is alienated from himself, from his fellow men, and from nature.[1] He has been transformed into a commodity, experiences his life forces as

[1] Cf. a more detailed discussion of the problem of alienation and of the influence of modern society on the character of man in E. Fromm *The Sane Society,* Rinehart & Company, New York, 1955.

an investment which must bring him the maximum profit obtainable under existing market conditions. Human relations are essentially those of alienated automatons, each basing his security on staying close to the herd, and not being different in thought, feeling or action. While everybody tries to be as close as possible to the rest, everybody remains utterly alone, pervaded by the deep sense of insecurity, anxiety and guilt which always results when human separateness cannot be overcome. Our civilization offers many palliatives which help people to be consciously unaware of this aloneness: first of all the strict routine of bureaucratized, mechanical work, which helps people to remain unaware of their most fundamental human desires, of the longing for transcendence and unity. Inasmuch as the routine alone does not succeed in this, man overcomes his unconscious despair by the routine of amusement, the passive consumption of sounds and sights offered by the amusement industry; furthermore by the satisfaction of buying ever new things, and soon exchanging them for others. Modern man is actually close to the picture Huxley describes in his *Brave New World:* well fed, well clad, satisfied sexually, yet without self, without any except the most superficial contact with his fellow men, guided by the slogans which Huxley formulated so succinctly, such as: "When the individual feels, the community reels"; or "Never put off till tomorrow the fun you can have today," or, as the crowning statement: "Everybody is happy nowadays." Man's happiness today consists in "having fun." Having fun lies in the satisfaction of consuming and "taking in" commodities, sights, food, drinks, cigarettes, people, lectures, books, movies—all are consumed, swallowed. The world is one great object for our appetite, a big apple, a big bottle, a big breast; we are the sucklers, the eternally expectant ones, the hopeful ones—and the eternally disappointed ones. Our character is geared to exchange and to receive, to barter and to consume; everything, spiritual as well as material objects, becomes an object of exchange and of consumption.

The situation as far as love is concerned corresponds, as it has to by necessity, to this social character of modern man. Automatons cannot love; they can exchange their "personality packages" and hope for a fair bargain. One of the most significant expressions of love, and especially of marriage with this alienated structure, is the idea of the "team." In any number of articles on happy marriage, the ideal described is that of the smoothly functioning team. This description is not too different from the idea of a smoothly functioning employee; he should be "reasonably independent," co-operative, tolerant, and at the same time ambitious and aggressive. Thus, the marriage counselor tells us, the husband should "understand" his wife and be helpful. He should comment favorably on her new dress, and on a tasty dish. She, in turn, should understand when he comes home tired and disgruntled, she should listen attentively when he talks about his business troubles, should not be angry but understanding when he forgets her birthday. All this kind of relationship amounts to is the well-oiled relationship between two persons who remain strangers all their lives, who never arrive at a "central relationship," but who treat each other with courtesy and who attempt to make each other feel better.

In this concept of love and marriage the main emphasis is on finding a refuge from an otherwise unbearable sense of aloneness. In "love" one has found, at last, a haven from aloneness. One forms an alliance of two against the world, and this egoism *à deux* is mistaken for love and intimacy.

The emphasis on team spirit, mutual tolerance and so forth is a relatively recent development. It was preceded, in the years after the First World War, by a concept of love in which mutual sexual satisfaction was supposed to be the basis for satisfactory love relations, and especially for a happy marriage. It was believed that the reasons for the frequent unhappiness in marriage were to be found in that the marriage partners had not made a correct "sexual adjustment"; the reason for this fault was seen in the ignorance regarding "correct" sexual behavior, hence in the faulty sexual technique of one or both partners. In order to "cure" this fault, and to help the unfortunate couples who could not love each other, many books gave instructions and counsel concerning the correct sexual behavior, and promised implicitly or explicitly that happiness and love would follow. The underlying idea was that love is the child of sexual pleasure, and that if two people learn how to satisfy each other sexually, they will love each other. It fitted the general illusion of the time to assume that using the right techniques is the solution not only to technical problems of industrial production, but of all human problems as well. One ignored the fact that the contrary of the underlying assumption is true.

Love is not the result of adequate sexual satisfaction, but sexual happiness—even the knowledge of the so-called sexual technique—is the result of love. If aside from everyday observation this thesis needed to be proved, such proof can be found in ample material of psychoanalytic data. The study of the most frequent sexual problems—frigidity in women, and the more or less severe forms of psychic impotence in men—shows that the cause does not lie in a lack of knowledge of the right technique, but in the inhibitions which make it impossible to love. Fear of or hatred for the other sex are at the bottom of those difficulties which prevent a person from giving himself completely, from acting spontaneously, from trusting the sexual partner in the immediacy and directness of physical closeness. If a sexually inhibited person can emerge from fear or hate, and hence become capable of loving, his or her sexual problems are solved. If not, no amount of knowledge about sexual techniques will help.

But while the data of psychoanalytic therapy point to the fallacy of the idea that knowledge of the correct sexual technique leads to sexual happiness and love, the underlying assumption that love is the concomitant of mutual sexual satisfaction was largely influenced by the theories of Freud. For Freud, love was basically a sexual phenomenon. "Man having found by experience that sexual (genital) love afforded him his greatest gratification, so that it became in fact a prototype of all happiness to him, must have been thereby impelled to seek his happiness further along the path of sexual relations, to make genital eroticism the central point of his life."[2] The experience of brotherly love is, for Freud, an outcome of sexual desire, but with the sexual instinct being transformed into an impulse with "inhibited aim." "Love with an inhibited aim was indeed originally full of sensual love, and in man's unconscious mind is so still."[3] As far as the feeling of fusion, of oneness ("oceanic feeling"), which is the essence of mystical experience and the root of the most intense sense of union with one other person or with one's fellow men, is concerned, it was interpreted by Freud as a pathological phenomenon, as a regression to a state of an early "limitless narcissism."[4]

It is only one step further that for Freud love is in itself an irrational phenomenon. The difference between irrational

[2]S. Freud, *Civilization and Its Discontents,* translated by J. Riviere, The Hogarth Press, Ltd., London, 1953, p. 69.

[3]*Ibid.,* p. 69.

[4]*Ibid.,* p. 21.

love, and love as an expression of the mature personality does not exist for him. He pointed out in a paper on transference love,[5] that transference love is essentially not different from the "normal" phenomenon of love. Falling in love always verges on the abnormal, is always accompanied by blindness to reality, compulsiveness, and is a transference from love objects of childhood. Love as a rational phenomenon, as the crowning achievement of maturity, was, to Freud, no subject matter for investigation, since it had no real existence.

However, it would be a mistake to overestimate the influence of Freud's ideas on the concept that love is the result of sexual attraction, or rather that it is the *same* as sexual satisfaction, reflected in conscious feeling. Essentially the causal nexus proceeds the other way around. Freud's ideas were partly influenced by the spirit of the nineteenth century; partly they became popular through the prevailing spirit of the years after the First World War. Some of the factors which influenced both the popular and the Freudian concepts were, first, the reaction against the strict mores of the Victorian age. The second factor determining Freud's theories lies in the prevailing concept of man, which is based on the structure of capitalism. In order to prove that capitalism corresponded to the natural needs of man, one had to show that man was by nature competitive and full of mutual hostility. While economists "proved" this in terms of the insatiable desire for economic gain, and the Darwinists in terms of the biological law of the survival of the fittest, Freud came to the same result by the assumption that man is driven by a limitless desire for the sexual conquest of all women, and that only the pressure of society prevented man from acting on his desires. As a result men are necessarily jealous of each other, and this mutual jealousy and competition would con-

[5]Freud, *Gesamte Werke,* London, 1940–52, Vol. X.

tinue even if all social and economic reasons for it would disappear.[6]

Eventually, Freud was largely influenced in his thinking by the type of materialism prevalent in the nineteenth century. One believed that the substratum of all mental phenomena was to be found in physiological phenomena; hence love, hate, ambition, jealousy were explained by Freud as so many outcomes of various forms of the sexual instinct. He did not see that the basic reality lies in the totality of human existence, first of all in the human situation common to all men, and secondly in the practice of life determined by the specific structure of society. (The decisive step beyond this type of materialism was taken by Marx in his "historical materialism," in which not the body, nor an instinct like the need for food or possession, serves as the key to the understanding of man, but the total life process of man, his "practice of life.") According to Freud, the full and uninhibited satisfaction of all instinctual desires would create mental health and happiness. But the obvious clinical facts demonstrate that men— and women who devote their lives to unrestricted sexual satisfaction do not attain happiness, and very often suffer from severe neurotic conflicts or symptoms. The complete satisfaction of all instinctual needs is not only not a basis for happiness, it does not even guarantee sanity. Yet Freud's idea could only have become so popular in the period after the First World War because of the changes which had occurred in the spirit of capitalism, from the emphasis on saving to that on spending, from self-frustration as a means for economic success to consumption as the basis for an ever-widening market, and as the main satisfaction for the anx-

[6]The only pupil of Freud who never separated from the master, and yet who in the last years of his life changed his views on love, was Sándor Ferenczi. For an excellent discussion on this subject see *The Leaven of Love* by Izette de Forest, Harper & Brothers, New York, 1954.

ious, automatized individual. Not to postpone the satisfaction of any desire became the main tendency in the sphere of sex as well as in that of all material consumption.

It is interesting to compare the concepts of Freud, which correspond to the spirit of capitalism as it existed, yet unbroken, around the beginning of this century, with the theoretical concepts of one of the most brilliant contemporary psychoanalysts, the late H. S. Sullivan. In Sullivan's psychoanalytic system we find, in contrast to Freud's, a strict division between sexuality and love.

What is the meaning of love and intimacy in Sullivan's concept? "Intimacy is that type of situation involving two people which permits validation of all components of personal worth. Validation of personal worth requires a type of relationship which I call collaboration, by which I mean clearly formulated adjustments of one's behavior to the expressed needs of the other person in pursuit of increasingly identical—that is, more and more nearly mutual satisfactions, and in the maintenance of increasingly similar security operations."[7] If we free Sullivan's statement from its somewhat involved language, the essence of love is seen in a situation of collaboration, in which two people feel: "We play according to the rules of the game to preserve our prestige and feeling of superiority and merit."[8]

[7] H. S. Sullivan, *The Interpersonal Theory of Psychiatry*, W. W. Norton & Co., New York, 1953, p. 246. It must be noted that although Sullivan gives this definition in connection with the strivings of pre-adolescence, he speaks of them as integrating tendencies, coming out during pre-adolescence, "which when they are completely developed, we call love," and says that this love in pre-adolescence "represents the beginning of something very like full-blown, psychiatrically defined *love.*"

[8] *Ibid.*, p. 246. Another definition of love by Sullivan, that love begins when a person feels another person's needs to be as important as his own, is less colored by the marketing aspect than the above formulation.

Just as Freud's concept of love is a description of the experience of the patriarchal male in terms of nineteenth-century capitalism, Sullivan's description refers to the experience of the alienated, marketing personality of the twentieth century. It is a description of an "egotism *à deux*," of two people pooling their common interests, and standing together against a hostile and alienated world. Actually his definition of intimacy is in principle valid for the feeling of any cooperating team, in which everybody "adjusts his behavior to the expressed needs of the other person in the pursuit of common aims" (it is remarkable that Sullivan speaks here of *expressed* needs, when the least one could say about love is that it implies a reaction to *unexpressed* needs between two people).

Love as mutual sexual satisfaction, and love as "teamwork" and as a haven from aloneness, are the two "normal" forms of the disintegration of love in modern Western society, the socially patterned pathology of love. There are many individualized forms of the pathology of love, which result in conscious suffering and which are considered neurotic by psychiatrists and an increasing number of laymen alike. Some of the more frequent ones are briefly described in the following examples.

The basic condition for neurotic love lies in the fact that one or both of the "lovers" have remained attached to the figure of a parent, and transfer the feelings, expectations and fears one once had toward father or mother to the loved person in adult life; the persons involved have never emerged from a pattern of infantile relatedness, and seek for this pattern in their affective demands in adult life. In these cases, the person has remained, affectively, a child of two, or of five, or of twelve, while intellectually and socially he is on the level of his chronological age. In the more severe cases, this emotional immaturity leads to disturbances in his social effectiveness; in the less severe ones, the conflict is limited to the sphere of intimate personal relationships.

Referring to our previous discussion of the mother- or father-centered personality, the following example for this type of neurotic love relation to be found frequently today deals with men who in their emotional development have remained stuck in an infantile attachment to mother. These are men who have never been weaned as it were from mother. These men still feel like children; they want mother's protection, love, warmth, care, and admiration; they want mother's unconditional love, a love which is given for no other reason than that they need it, that they are mother's child, that they are helpless. Such men frequently are quite affectionate and charming if they try to induce a woman to love them, and even after they have succeeded in this. But their relationship to the woman (as, in fact, to all other people) remains superficial and irresponsible. Their aim is to be loved, not to love. There is usually a good deal of vanity in this type of man, more or less hidden grandiose ideas. If they have found the right woman, they feel secure, on top of the world, and can display a great deal of affection and charm, and this is the reason why these men are often so deceptive. But when, after a while, the woman does not continue to live up to their phantastic expectations, conflicts and resentment start to develop. If the woman is not always admiring them, if she makes claims for a life of her own, if she wants to be loved and protected herself, and in extreme cases, if she is not willing to condone his love affairs with other women (or even have an admiring interest in them), the man feels deeply hurt and disappointed, and usually rationalizes this feeling with the idea that the woman "does not love him, is selfish, or is domineering." Anything short of the attitude of a loving mother toward a charming child is taken as proof of a lack of love. These men usually confuse their affectionate behavior, their wish to please, with genuine love and thus arrive at the conclusion that they are being treated quite unfairly; they imagine themselves to be the great lovers and complain bitterly about the ingratitude of their love partner.

In rare cases such a mother-centered person can function without any severe disturbances. If his mother, in fact, "loved" him in an overprotective manner (perhaps being domineering, but without being destructive), if he finds a wife of the same motherly type, if his special gifts and talents permit him to use his charm and be admired (as is the case sometimes with successful politicians), he is "well adjusted" in a social sense, without ever reaching a higher level of maturity. But under less favorable conditions—and these are naturally more frequent—his love life, if not his social life, will be a serious disappointment; conflicts, and frequently intense anxiety and depression arise when this type of personality is left alone.

In a still more severe form of pathology the fixation to mother is deeper and more irrational. On this level, the wish is not, symbolically speaking, to return to mother's protecting arms, nor to her nourishing breast, but to her all-receiving—and all-destroying—womb. If the nature of sanity is to grow out of the womb into the world, the nature of severe mental disease is to be attracted by the womb, to be sucked back into it—and that is to be taken away from life. This kind of fixation usually occurs in relation to mothers who relate themselves to their children in this swallowing-destroying way. Sometimes in the name of love, sometimes of duty, they want to keep the child, the adolescent, the man, within them; he should not be able to breathe but through them; not be able to love, except on a superficial sexual level—degrading all other women; he should not be able to be free and independent but an eternal cripple or a criminal.

This aspect of mother, the destructive, engulfing one, is the negative aspect of the mother figure. Mother can give life, and she can take life. She is the one to revive, and the one to destroy; she can do miracles of love—and nobody can hurt more than she. In religious images (such as the Hindu goddess Kali) and in dream symbolism the two opposite aspects of mother can often be found.

A different form of neurotic pathology is to be found in such cases where the main attachment is that to father.

A case in point is a man whose mother is cold and aloof, while his father (partly as a result of his wife's coldness) concentrates all his affection and interest on the son. He is a "good father," but at the same time authoritarian. Whenever he is pleased with the son's conduct he praises him, gives him presents, is affectionate; whenever the son displeases him, he withdraws, or scolds. The son, for whom father's affection is the only one he has, becomes attached to father in a slavish way. His main aim in life is to please father—and when he succeeds he feels happy, secure and satisfied. But when he makes a mistake, fails, or does not succeed in pleasing father, he feels deflated, unloved, cast out. In later life such a man will try to find a father figure to whom he attaches himself in a similar fashion. His whole life becomes a sequence of ups and downs, depending on whether he has succeeded in winning father's praise. Such men are often very successful in their social careers. They are conscientious, reliable, eager— provided their chosen father image understands how to handle them. But in their relationships to women they remain aloof and distant. The woman is of no central significance to them; they usually have a slight contempt for her, often masked as the fatherly concern for a little girl. They may have impressed a woman initially by their masculine quality, but they become increasingly disappointing, when the woman they marry discovers that she is destined to play a secondary role to the primary affection for the father figure who is prominent in the husband's life at any given time; that is, unless the wife happens to have remained attached to her father—and thus is happy with a husband who relates to her as to a capricious child.

More complicated is the kind of neurotic disturbance in love which is based on a different kind of parental situation, occurring when parents do not love each other, but are too restrained to quarrel or to indicate any signs of dissatisfaction outwardly. At the same time, remoteness makes them also unspontaneous in their relationship to their children. What a little girl experiences is an atmosphere of "correctness," but one which never permits a close contact with either father or mother, and hence leaves the girl puzzled and afraid. She is never sure of what the parents feel or think; there is always an element of the unknown, the mysterious, in the atmosphere. As a result the girl withdraws into a world of her own, daydreams, remains remote, and retains the same attitude in her love relationships later on.

Furthermore the withdrawal results in the development of intense anxiety, a feeling of not being firmly grounded in the world, and often leads to masochistic tendencies as the only way to experience intense excitement. Often such women would prefer having the husband make a scene and shout, to his maintaining a more normal and sensible behavior, because at least it would take away the burden of tension and fear from them; not so rarely they unconsciously provoke such behavior, in order to end the tormenting suspense of affective neutrality.

Other frequent forms of irrational love are described in the following paragraphs, without going into an analysis of the specific factors in childhood development which are at their roots:

A form of pseudo-love which is not infrequent and is often experienced (and more often described in moving pictures and novels) as the "great love" is *idolatrous love*. If a person has not reached the level where he has a sense of identity, of I-ness, rooted in the productive unfolding of his own powers, he tends to "idolize" the loved person. He is alienated from his own powers and projects them into the loved person, who is worshiped as the *summum bonum,* the bearer of all love, all light, all bliss. In this process he deprives himself of all sense of strength, loses himself in the loved one instead of finding himself. Since usually no person can, in the long run, live up to the expectations of her (or his) idolatrous worshiper, disappointment is bound to occur, and as a remedy a new idol is sought for, sometimes in an unending circle. What is characteristic for this type of idolatrous love is, at the beginning, the intensity and suddenness of the love experience. This idolatrous love is often described as the true, great love; but while it is meant to portray the intensity and depth of love, it only demonstrates the hunger and despair of the idolator. Needless to say it is not rare that two persons find each other in a mutual idolatry which, sometimes, in extreme cases, represents the picture of a *folie à deux*.

Another form of pseudo-love is what may be called *"sentimental love."* Its essence lies in the fact that love is experienced only in phantasy and not in the here-and-now relationship to another person who is real. The most widespread form of this type of love is that to be found in the vicarious love satisfaction experienced by the consumer of screen pictures, magazine love stories and love songs. All the unfulfilled desires for love, union, and closeness find their satisfaction in the consumption of these products. A man and a woman who in relation to their spouses are incapable of ever penetrating

the wall of separateness are moved to tears when they participate in the happy or unhappy love story of the couple on the
screen. For many couples, seeing these stories on the screen
is the only occasion on which they experience love—not for
each other, but together, as spectators of other people's
"love." As long as love is a daydream, they can participate;
as soon as it comes down to the reality of the relationship
between two real people—they are frozen.

Another aspect of sentimental love is the abstractification
of love in terms of time. A couple may be deeply moved by
memories of their past love, although when this past was
present no love was experienced—or the phantasies of their
future love. How many engaged or newly married couples
dream of their bliss of love to take place in the future, while
at the very moment at which they live they are already
beginning to be bored with each other? This tendency coin-
cides with a general attitude characteristic of modern man.
He lives in the past or in the future, but not in the present.
He remembers sentimentally his childhood and his mother—
or he makes happy plans for the future. Whether love is
experienced vicariously by participating in the fictitious experiences of others, or whether it is shifted away from the
present to the past or the future, this abstractified and alienated form of love serves as an opiate which alleviates the pain
of reality, the aloneness and separateness of the individual.

Still another form of neurotic love lies in the use of *projective mechanisms* for the purpose of avoiding one's own problems, and being concerned with the defects and frailties of
the "loved" person instead. Individuals behave in this respect very much as groups, nations or religions do. They have
a fine appreciation for even the minor shortcomings of the
other person, and go blissfully ahead ignoring their own—
always busy trying to accuse or to reform the other person.
If two people both do it—as is so often the case—the relation-

ship of love becomes transformed into one of mutual projection. If I am domineering or indecisive, or greedy, I accuse my partner of it, and depending on my character, I either want to cure him or to punish him. The other person does the same—and both thus succeed in ignoring their own problems and hence fail to undertake any steps which would help them in their own development.

Another form of projection is the projection of one's own problems on the children. First of all such projection takes place not infrequently in the wish for children. In such cases the wish for children is primarily determined by projecting one's own problem of existence on that of the children. When a person feels that he has not been able to make sense of his own life, he tries to make sense of it in terms of the life of his children. But one is bound to fail within oneself *and* for the children. The former because the problem of existence can be solved by each one only for himself, and not by proxy; the latter because one lacks in the very qualities which one needs to guide the children in their own search for an answer. Children serve for projective purposes also when the question arises of dissolving an unhappy marriage. The stock argument of parents in such a situation is that they cannot separate in order not to deprive the children of the blessings of a unified home. Any detailed study would show, however, that the atmosphere of tension and unhappiness within the "unified family" is more harmful to the children than an open break would be—which teaches them at least that man is able to end an intolerable situation by a courageous decision.

One other frequent error must be mentioned here. The illusion, namely, that love means necessarily the absence of conflict. Just as it is customary for people to believe that pain and sadness should be avoided under all circumstances, they believe that love means the absence of any conflict. And they find good reasons for this idea in the fact that the struggles around them seem only to be destructive interchanges which bring no good to either one of those concerned. But the reason for this lies in the fact that the "conflicts" of most people are actually attempts to avoid the *real* conflicts. They are disagreements on minor or superficial matters which by their very nature do not lend themselves to clarification or solution. Real conflicts between two people, those which do not serve to cover up or to project, but which are experienced on the deep level of inner reality to which they belong, are not destructive. They lead to clarification, they produce a catharsis from which both persons emerge with more knowledge and more strength. This leads us to emphasize again something said above.

Love is possible only if two persons communicate with each other from the center of their existence, hence if each one of them experiences himself from the center of his existence. Only in this "central experience" is human reality, only here is aliveness, only here is the basis for love. Love, experienced thus, is a constant challenge; it is not a resting place, but a moving, growing, working together; even whether there is harmony or conflict, joy or sadness, is secondary to the fundamental fact that two people experience themselves from the essence of their existence, that they are one with each other by being one with themselves, rather than by fleeing from themselves. There is only one proof for the presence of love: the depth of the relationship, and the aliveness and strength in each person concerned; this is the fruit by which love is recognized.

Just as automatons cannot love each other they cannot love God. The *disintegration of the love of God* has reached the same proportions as the disintegration of the love of man. This fact is in blatant contradiction to the idea that we are witnessing a religious renaissance in this epoch. Nothing could be further from the truth. What we witness (even though there are exceptions) is a regression to an idolatric concept of God, and a transformation of the love of God into a relationship fitting an alienated character structure. The regression to an idolatric concept of God is easy to see. People are anxious, without principles or faith, they find themselves without an aim except the one to move ahead; hence they continue to remain children, to hope for father or mother to come to their help when help is needed.

True, in religious cultures, like that of the Middle Ages, the average man also looked at God as to a helping father and mother. But at the same time he took God seriously also, in the sense that the paramount goal of his life was to live according to God's principles, to make "salvation" the supreme concern to which all other activities were subordinated. Today, nothing of such effort is present. Daily life is strictly separated from any religious values. It is devoted to the striving for material comforts, and for success on the personality market. The principles on which our secular efforts are built are those of indifference and egotism (the latter often labeled as "individualism," or "individual initiative"). Man of truly religious cultures may be compared with children at the age of eight, who need father as a helper, but who begin to adopt his teachings and principles in their lives. Contemporary man is rather like a child of three, who cries for father when he needs him, and otherwise is quite self-sufficient when he can play.

In this respect, in the infantile dependence on an anthropomorphic picture of God without the transformation of life according to the principles of God, we are closer to a primitive idolatric tribe than to the religious culture of the Middle Ages. In another respect our religious situation shows features which are new, and characteristic only of contemporary Western capitalistic society. I can refer to statements made in a previous part of this book. Modern man has transformed himself into a commodity; he experiences his life energy as an investment with which he should make the highest profit, considering his position and the situation on the personality market. He is alienated from himself, from his fellow men and from nature. His main aim is profitable exchange of his skills, knowledge, and of himself, his "personality package" with others who are equally intent on a fair and profitable exchange. Life has no goal except the one to move, no principle except the one of fair exchange, no satisfaction except the one to consume.

What can the concept of God mean under these circumstances? It is transformed from its original religious meaning into one fitting the alienated culture of success. In the religious revival of recent times, the belief in God has been transformed into a psychological device to make one better fitted for the competitive struggle.

Religion allies itself with auto-suggestion and psychotherapy to help man in his business activities. In the twenties one had not yet called upon God for purposes of "improving one's personality." The best-seller in the year 1938, Dale Carnegie's *How to Win Friends and Influence People,* remained on a strictly secular level. What was the function of Carnegie's book at that time is the function of our greatest best-seller today, *The Power of Positive Thinking* by the Reverend N. V. Peale. In this religious book it is not even questioned whether our dominant concern with success is in itself in accordance with the spirit of monotheistic religion. On the contrary, this supreme aim is never doubted, but belief in God and prayer is recommended as a means to increase one's ability to be successful. Just as modern psychiatrists recommend happiness of the employee, in order to be more appealing to the customers, some ministers recommend love of God in order to be more successful. "Make God your partner" means to make God a partner in business, rather than to become one with Him in love, justice and truth. Just as brotherly love has been replaced by impersonal fairness, God has been transformed into a remote General Director of Universe, Inc.; you know that he is there, he runs the show (although it would probably run without him too), you never see him, but you acknowledge his leadership while you are "doing your part."

IV

THE PRACTICE OF LOVE

Having dealt with the theoretical aspect of the art of loving, we now are confronted with a much more difficult problem, that of the *practice of the art of loving.* Can anything be learned about the practice of an art, except by practicing it?

The difficulty of the problem is enhanced by the fact that most people today, hence many readers of this book, expect to be given prescriptions of "how to do it yourself," and that means in our case to be taught how to love. I am afraid that anyone who approaches this last chapter in this spirit will be gravely disappointed. To love is a personal experience which everyone can only have by and for himself; in fact, there is hardly anybody who has not had this experience in a rudimentary way, at least, as a child, an adolescent, an adult. What the discussion of the practice of love can do is to discuss the premises of the art of loving, the approaches to it as it were, and the practice of these premises and approaches. The steps toward the goal can be practiced only by oneself,

97

and discussion ends before the decisive step is taken. Yet, I believe that the discussion of the approaches may be helpful for the mastery of the art—for those at least who have freed themselves from expecting "prescriptions."

The practice of any art has certain general requirements, quite regardless of whether we deal with the art of carpentry, medicine, or the art of love. First of all, the practice of an art requires *discipline*. I shall never be good at anything if I do not do it in a disciplined way; anything I do only if "I am in the mood" may be a nice or amusing hobby, but I shall never become a master in that art. But the problem is not only that of discipline in the practice of the particular art (say practicing every day a certain amount of hours) but it is that of discipline in one's whole life. One might think that nothing is easier to learn for modern man than discipline. Does he not spend eight hours a day in a most disciplined way at a job which is strictly routinized? The fact, however, is that modern man has exceedingly little self-discipline outside of the sphere of work. When he does not work, he wants to be lazy, to slouch or, to use a nicer word, to "relax." This very wish for laziness is largely a reaction against the routinization of life. Just because man is forced for eight hours a day to spend his energy for purposes not his own, in ways not his own, but prescribed for him by the rhythm of the work, he rebels and his rebelliousness takes the form of an infantile self-indulgence. In addition, in the battle against authoritarianism he has become distrustful of all discipline, of that enforced by irrational authority, as well as of rational discipline imposed by himself. Without such discipline, however, life becomes shattered, chaotic, and lacks in concentration.

That *concentration* is a necessary condition for the mastery of an art is hardly necessary to prove. Anyone who ever tried to learn an art knows this. Yet, even more than self-discipline, concentration is rare in our culture. On the contrary, our culture leads to an unconcentrated and diffused mode of life, hardly paralleled anywhere else. You do many things at once; you read, listen to the radio, talk, smoke, eat, drink. You are the consumer with the open mouth, eager and ready to swallow everything—pictures, liquor, knowledge. This lack of concentration is clearly shown in our difficulty in being alone with ourselves. To sit still, without talking, smoking, reading, drinking, is impossible for most people. They become nervous and fidgety, and must do something with their mouth or their hands. (Smoking is one of the symptoms of this lack of concentration; it occupies hand, mouth, eye and nose.)

A third factor is *patience*. Again, anyone who ever tried to master an art knows that patience is necessary if you want to achieve anything. If one is after quick results, one never learns an art. Yet, for modern man, patience is as difficult to practice as discipline and concentration. Our whole industrial system fosters exactly the opposite: quickness. All our machines are designed for quickness: the car and airplane bring us quickly to our destination—and the quicker the better. The machine which can produce the same quantity in half the time is twice as good as the older and slower one. Of course, there are important economic reasons for this. But, as in so many other aspects, human values have become determined by economic values. What is good for machines must be good for man—so goes the logic. Modern man thinks he loses something—time—when he does not do things quickly; yet he does not know what to do with the time he gains—except kill it.

Eventually, a condition of learning any art is a *supreme concern* with the mastery of the art. If the art is not something of supreme importance, the apprentice will never learn it. He will remain, at best, a good dilettante, but will never become a master. This condition is as necessary for the art of loving as for any other art. It seems, though, as if the proportion between masters and dilettantes is more heavily weighted in favor of the dilettantes in the art of loving than is the case with other arts.

One more point must be made with regard to the general conditions of learning an art. One does not begin to learn an art directly, but indirectly, as it were. One must learn a great number of other—and often seemingly disconnected— things before one starts with the art itself. An apprentice in carpentry begins by learning how to plane wood; an apprentice in the art of piano playing begins by practicing scales; an apprentice in the Zen art of archery begins by doing breathing exercises.[1] If one wants to become a master in any art, one's whole life must be devoted to it, or at least related to it. One's own person becomes an instrument in the practice of the art, and must be kept fit, according to the specific functions it has to fulfill. With regard to the art of loving, this means that anyone who aspires to become a master in this art must begin by *practicing* discipline, concentration and patience throughout every phase of his life.

How does one practice discipline? Our grandfathers would have been much better equipped to answer this question. Their recommendation was to get up early in the morning, not to indulge in unnecessary luxuries, to work hard. This type of discipline had obvious shortcomings. It was rigid and authoritarian, was centered around the virtues of frugality and saving, and in many ways was hostile to life. But in a reaction to this kind of discipline, there has been an increasing tendency to be suspicious of *any* discipline, and to make undisciplined, lazy indulgence in the rest of one's life the

[1]For a picture of the concentration, discipline, patience and concern necessary for the learning of an art, I want to refer the reader to *Zen in the Art of Archery,* by E. Herrigel, Pantheon Books, Inc., New York, 1953.

counterpart and balance for the routinized way of life imposed on us during the eight hours of work. To get up at a regular hour, to devote a regular amount of time during the day to activities such as meditating, reading, listening to music, walking; not to indulge, at least not beyond a certain minimum, in escapist activities like mystery stories and movies, not to overeat or overdrink are some obvious and rudimentary rules. It is essential, however, that discipline should not be practiced like a rule imposed on oneself from the outside, but that it becomes an expression of one's own will; that it is felt as pleasant, and that one slowly accustoms oneself to a kind of behavior which one would eventually miss, if one stopped practicing it. It is one of the unfortunate aspects of our Western concept of discipline (as of every virtue) that its practice is supposed to be somewhat painful and only if it is painful can it be "good." The East has recognized long ago that that which is good for man—for his body and for his soul—must also be agreeable, even though at the beginning some resistances must be overcome.

Concentration is by far more difficult to practice in our culture, in which everything seems to act against the ability to concentrate. The most important step in learning concentration is to learn to be alone with oneself without reading, listening to the radio, smoking or drinking. Indeed, to be able to concentrate means to be able to be alone with oneself—and this ability is precisely a condition for the ability to love. If I am attached to another person because I cannot stand on my own feet, he or she may be a lifesaver, but the relationship is not one of love. Paradoxically, the ability to be alone is the condition for the ability to love. Anyone who tries to be alone with himself will discover how difficult it is. He will begin to feel restless, fidgety, or even to sense considerable anxiety. He will be prone to rationalize his unwillingness to go on with this practice by thinking that it has no value, is just silly, that it takes too much time, and so on, and so on. He will also observe that all sorts of thoughts come to his mind which take possession of him. He will find himself thinking about his plans for later in the day, or about some difficulty in a job he has to do, or where to go in the evening, or about any number of things that will fill his mind—rather than permitting it to empty itself. It would be helpful to practice a few very simple exercises, as, for instance, to sit in a relaxed position (neither slouching, nor rigid), to close one's eyes, and to try to see a white screen in front of one's eyes, and to try to remove all interfering pictures and thoughts, then to try to follow one's breathing; not to think about it, nor force it, but to follow it—and in doing so to sense it; furthermore to try to have a sense of "I"; I = myself, as the center of my powers, as the creator of my world. One should, at least, do such a concentration exercise every morning for twenty minutes (and if possible longer) and every evening before going to bed.[2]

Besides such exercises, one must learn to be concentrated in everything one does, in listening to music, in reading a book, in talking to a person, in seeing a view. The activity at this very moment must be the only thing that matters, to which one is fully given. If one is concentrated, it matters little *what* one is doing; the important, as well as the unimportant things assume a new dimension of reality, because they have one's full attention. To learn concentration requires avoiding, as far as possible, trivial conversation, that is, conversation which is not genuine. If two people talk about the growth of a tree they both know, or about the taste of the

[2]While there is a considerable amount of theory and practice on this point in the Eastern, especially the Indian cultures, similar aims have been followed in recent years also in the West. The most significant, in my opinion, is the school of Gindler, the aim of which is the sensing of one's body. For the understanding of the Gindler method, cf. also Charlotte Selver's work, in her lectures and courses at the New School, in New York.

bread they have just eaten together, or about a common experience in their job, such conversation can be relevant, provided they experience what they are talking about, and do not deal with it in an abstractified way; on the other hand, a conversation can deal with matters of politics or religion and yet be trivial; this happens when the two people talk in clichés, when their hearts are not in what they are saying. I should add here that just as it is important to avoid trivial conversation, it is important to avoid bad company. By bad company I do not refer only to people who are vicious and destructive; one should avoid their company because their orbit is poisonous and depressing. I mean also the company of zombies, of people whose soul is dead, although their body is alive; of people whose thoughts and conversation are trivial; who chatter instead of talk, and who assert cliché opinions instead of thinking. However, it is not always possible to avoid the company of such people, nor even necessary. If one does not react in the expected way—that is, in clichés and trivialities—but directly and humanly, one will often find that such people change their behavior, often helped by the surprise effected by the shock of the unexpected.

To be concentrated in relation to others means primarily to be able to listen. Most people listen to others, or even give advice, without really listening. They do not take the other person's talk seriously, they do not take their own answers seriously either. As a result, the talk makes them tired. They are under the illusion that they would be even more tired if they listened with concentration. But the opposite is true. Any activity, if done in a concentrated fashion, makes one more awake (although afterward natural and beneficial tiredness sets in), while every unconcentrated activity makes one sleepy—while at the same time it makes it difficult to fall asleep at the end of the day.

To be concentrated means to live fully in the present, in

the here and now, and not to think of the next thing to be done, while I am doing something right now. Needless to say that concentration must be practiced most of all by people who love each other. They must learn to be close to each other without running away in the many ways in which this is customarily done. The beginning of the practice of concentration will be difficult; it will appear as if one could never achieve the aim. That this implies the necessity to have patience need hardly be said. If one does not know that everything has its time, and wants to force things, then indeed one will never succeed in becoming concentrated—nor in the art of loving. To have an idea of what patience is one need only watch a child learning to walk. It falls, falls again, and falls again, and yet it goes on trying, improving, until one day it walks without falling. What could the grown-up person achieve if he had the child's patience and its concentration in the pursuits which are important to him!

One cannot learn to concentrate without becoming *sensitive to oneself.* What does this mean? Should one think about oneself all the time, "analyze" oneself, or what? If we were to talk about being sensitive to a machine, there would be little difficulty in explaining what is meant. Anybody, for instance, who drives a car is sensitive to it. Even a small, unaccustomed noise is noticed, and so is a small change in the pickup of the motor. In the same way, the driver is sensitive to changes in the road surface, to movements of the cars before and behind him. Yet, he is not *thinking about* all these factors; his mind is in a state of relaxed alertness, open to all relevant changes in the situation on which he is concentrated—that of driving his car safely.

If we look at the situation of being sensitive to another human being, we find the most obvious example in the sensitiveness and responsiveness of a mother to her baby. She notices certain bodily changes, demands, anxieties, before they are overtly expressed. She wakes up because of her child's crying, where another and much louder sound would not waken her. All this means that she is sensitive to the manifestations of the child's life; she is not anxious or worried, but in a state of alert equilibrium, receptive to any significant communication coming from the child. In the same way one can be sensitive toward oneself. One is aware, for instance, of a sense of tiredness or depression, and instead of giving in to it and supporting it by depressive thoughts which are always at hand, one asks oneself "what happened?" Why am I depressed? The same is done by noticing when one is irritated or angry, or tending to daydreaming, or other escape activities. In each of these instances the important thing is to be aware of them, and not to rationalize them in the thousand and one ways in which this can be done; furthermore, to be open to our own inner voice, which will tell us—often rather immediately—why we are anxious, depressed, irritated.

The average person has a sensitivity toward his bodily processes; he notices changes, or even small amounts of pain; this kind of bodily sensitivity is relatively easy to experience because most persons have an image of how it feels to be well. The same sensitivity toward one's mental processes is much more difficult, because many people have never known a person who functions optimally. They take the psychic functioning of their parents and relatives, or of the social group they have been born into, as the norm, and as long as they do not differ from these they feel normal and without interest in observing anything. There are many people, for instance, who have never seen a loving person, or a person with integrity, or courage, or concentration. It is quite obvious that in order to be sensitive to oneself, one has to have an image of complete, healthy human functioning—and how is one to acquire such an experience if one has not had it in one's own childhood, or later in life? There is certainly no simple answer to this question; but the question points to one very critical factor in our educational system.

While we teach knowledge, we are losing that teaching which is the most important one for human development: the teaching which can only be given by the simple presence of a mature, loving person. In previous epochs of our own culture, or in China and India, the man most highly valued was the person with outstanding spiritual qualities. Even the teacher was not only, or even primarily, a source of information, but his function was to convey certain human attitudes. In contemporary capitalistic society—and the same holds true for Russian Communism—the men suggested for admiration and emulation are everything but bearers of significant spiritual qualities. Those are essentially in the public eye who give the average man a sense of vicarious satisfaction. Movie stars, radio entertainers, columnists, important business or government figures—these are the models for emulation. Their main qualification for this function is often that they have succeeded in making the news. Yet, the situation does not seem to be altogether hopeless. If one considers the fact that a man like Albert Schweitzer could become famous in the United States, if one visualizes the many possibilities to make our youth familiar with living and historical personalities who show what human beings can achieve as human beings, and not as entertainers (in the broad sense of the word), if one thinks of the great works of literature and art of all ages, there seems to be a chance of creating a vision of good human functioning, and hence of sensitivity to malfunctioning. If we should not succeed in keeping alive a vision of mature life, then indeed we are confronted with the probability that our whole cultural tradition will break down. This tradition is not primarily based on the transmission of certain kinds of knowledge, but of certain kinds of human traits. If the coming generations will not see these traits any more, a five-thousand-year-old culture will break down, even if its knowledge is transmitted and further developed.

Thus far I have discussed what is needed for the practice of *any* art. Now I shall discuss those qualities which are of specific significance for the ability to love. According to what I said about the nature of love, the main condition for the achievement of love is the *overcoming* of one's *narcissism*. The narcissistic orientation is one in which one experiences as real only that which exists within oneself, while the phenomena in the outside world have no reality in themselves, but are experienced only from the viewpoint of their being useful or dangerous to one. The opposite pole to narcissism is objectivity; it is the faculty to see people and things *as they are*, objectively, and to be able to separate this *objective* picture from a picture which is formed by one's desires and fears. All forms of psychosis show the inability to be objective, to an extreme degree. For the insane person the only reality that exists is that within him, that of his fears and desires. He sees the world outside as symbols of his inner world, as his creation. All of us do the same when we dream. In the dream we produce events, we stage dramas, which are the expression of our wishes and fears (although sometimes also of our insights and judgment), and while we are asleep we are convinced that the product of our dreams is as real as the reality which we perceive in our waking state.

The insane person or the dreamer fails *completely* in having an objective view of the world outside; but all of us are more or less insane, or more or less asleep; all of us have an unobjective view of the world, one which is distorted by our narcissistic orientation. Do I need to give examples? Anyone can find them easily by watching himself, his neighbors, and by reading the newspapers. They vary in the degree of the narcissistic distortion of reality. A woman, for instance, calls up the doctor, saying she wants to come to his office that same afternoon. The doctor answers that he is not free this same afternoon, but that he can see her the next day. Her answer is: But, doctor, I live only five minutes from your office. She cannot understand his explanation that it does not save *him* time that for her the distance is so short. She experiences the situation narcissistically: since *she* saves time, *he* saves times; the only reality to her is she herself.

Less extreme—or perhaps only less obvious—are the distortions which are commonplace in interpersonal relations. How many parents experience the child's reactions in terms of his being obedient, of giving them pleasure, of being a credit to them, and so forth, instead of perceiving or even being interested in what the child feels for and by himself? How many husbands have a picture of their wives as being domineering, because their own attachment to mother makes them interpret any demand as a restriction of their freedom? How many wives think their husbands are ineffective or stupid, because they do not live up to a phantasy picture of a shining knight which they might have built up as children?

The lack of objectivity, as far as foreign nations are concerned, is notorious. From one day to another, another nation is made out to be utterly depraved and fiendish, while one's own nation stands for everything that is good and noble. Every action of the enemy is judged by one standard—every action of oneself by another. Even good deeds by the enemy are considered a sign of particular devilishness, meant to deceive us and the world, while our bad deeds are necessary and justified by our noble goals which they serve. Indeed, if one examines the relationship between nations, as well as between individuals, one comes to the conclusion that objectivity is the exception, and a greater or lesser degree of narcissistic distortion is the rule.

The faculty to think objectively is *reason;* the emotional attitude behind reason is that of *humility.* To be objective, to use one's reason, is possible only if one has achieved an attitude of humility, if one has emerged from the dreams of omniscience and omnipotence which one has as a child.

In terms of this discussion of the practice of the art of loving, this means: love being dependent on the relative absence of narcissism, it requires the development of humility, objectivity and reason. One's whole life must be devoted to this aim. Humility and objectivity are indivisible, just as love is. I cannot be truly objective about my family if I cannot be objective about the stranger, and vice versa. If I want to learn the art of loving, I must strive for objectivity in every situation, and become sensitive to the situations where I am not objective. I must try to see the difference between *my* picture of a person and his behavior, as it is narcissistically distorted, and the person's reality as it exists regardless of my interests, needs and fears. To have acquired the capacity for objectivity and reason is half the road to achieving the art of loving, but it must be acquired with regard to everybody with whom one comes in contact. If someone would want to reserve his objectivity for the loved person, and think he can dispense with it in his relationship to the rest of the world, he will soon discover that he fails both here and there.

The ability to love depends on one's capacity to emerge from narcissism, and from the incestuous fixation to mother and clan; it depends on our capacity to grow, to develop a productive orientation in our relationship toward the world and ourselves. This process of emergence, of birth, of waking up, requires one quality as a necessary condition: *faith.* The practice of the art of loving requires the practice of faith.

What is faith? Is faith necessarily a matter of belief in God, or in religious doctrines? Is faith by necessity in contrast to, or divorced from, reason and rational thinking? Even to begin to understand the problem of faith one must differentiate between *rational* and *irrational faith.* By irrational faith I understand the belief (in a person or an idea) which is based on one's submission to irrational authority. In contrast, rational faith is a conviction which is rooted in one's own experience of thought or feeling. Rational faith is not primarily belief in something, but the quality of certainty and firmness which our convictions have. Faith is a character trait pervading the whole personality, rather than a specific belief.

Rational faith is rooted in productive intellectual and emotional activity. In rational thinking, in which faith is supposed to have no place, rational faith is an important component. How does the scientist, for instance, arrive at a new discovery? Does he start with making experiment after experiment, gathering fact after fact, without having a vision of what he expects to find? Rarely has a truly important discovery in any field been made in this way. Nor have people arrived at important conclusions when they were merely chasing a phantasy. The process of creative thinking in any field of human endeavor often starts with what may be called a "rational vision," itself a result of considerable previous study, reflective thinking, and observation. When the scientist succeeds in gathering enough data, or in working out a mathematical formulation to make his original vision highly plausible, he may be said to have arrived at a tentative hypothesis. A careful analysis of the hypothesis in order to discern its implications, and the amassing of data which support it, lead to a more adequate hypothesis and eventually perhaps to its inclusion in a wide-ranging theory.

The history of science is replete with instances of faith in reason and visions of truth. Copernicus, Kepler, Galileo, and Newton were all imbued with an unshakable faith in reason. For this Bruno was burned at the stake and Spinoza suffered excommunication. At every step from the conception of a rational vision to the formulation of a theory, *faith* is necessary: faith in the vision as a rationally valid aim to pursue, faith in the hypothesis as a likely and plausible proposition, and faith in the final theory, at least until a general consensus about its validity has been reached. This faith is rooted in one's own experience, in the confidence in one's power of thought, observation, and judgment. While irrational faith is the acceptance of something as true only *because* an authority or the majority say so, rational faith is rooted in an independent conviction based upon one's own productive observing and thinking, *in spite of* the majority's opinion.

Thought and judgment are not the only realm of experience in which rational faith is manifested. In the sphere of human relations, faith is an indispensable quality of any significant friendship or love. "Having faith" in another person means to be certain of the reliability and unchangeability of his fundamental attitudes, of the core of his personality, of his love. By this I do not mean that a person may not change his opinions, but that his basic motivations remain the same; that, for instance, his respect for life and human dignity is part of himself, not subject to change.

In the same sense we have faith in ourselves. We are aware of the existence of a self, of a core in our personality which is unchangeable and which persists throughout our life in spite of varying circumstances, and regardless of certain changes in opinions and feelings. It is this core which is the reality behind the word "I," and on which our conviction of our own identity is based. Unless we have faith in the persistence of our self, our feeling of identity is threatened and we become dependent on other people whose approval then becomes the basis for our feeling of identity. Only the person who has faith in himself is able to be faithful to others, because only he can be sure that he will be the same at a future time as he is today and, therefore, that he will feel and act as he now expects to. Faith in oneself is a condition of our ability to promise, and since, as Nietzsche said, man can be defined by his capacity to promise, faith is one of the conditions of human existence. What matters in relation to love is the faith in one's own love; in its ability to produce love in others, and in its reliability.

Another meaning of having faith in a person refers to the faith we have in the potentialities of others. The most rudimentary form in which this faith exists is the faith which the mother has toward her newborn baby: that it will live, grow, walk, and talk. However, the development of the child in this respect occurs with such regularity that the expectation of it does not seem to require faith. It is different with those potentialities which can fail to develop: the child's potentialities to love, to be happy, to use his reason, and more specific potentialities like artistic gifts. They are the seeds which grow and become manifest if the proper conditions for their development are given, and they can be stifled if there are absent.

One of the most important of these conditions is that the significant person in a child's life have faith in these potentialities. The presence of this faith makes the difference between education and manipulation. Education is identical with helping the child realize his potentialities.[3] The opposite of education is manipulation, which is based on the absence of faith in the growth of potentialities, and on the conviction that a child will be right only if the adults put into him what is desirable and suppress what seems to be undesirable. There is no need of faith in the robot, since there is no life in it either.

[3]The root of the word education is *e-ducere*, literally, to lead forth, or to bring out something which is potentially present.

The faith in others has its culmination in faith in *mankind*. In the Western world this faith was expressed in religious terms in the Judaeo-Christian religion, and in secular language it has found its strongest expression in the humanistic political and social ideas of the last hundred and fifty years. Like the faith in the child, it is based on the idea that the potentialities of man are such that given the proper conditions he will be capable of building a social order governed by the principles of equality, justice and love. Man has not yet achieved the building of such an order, and therefore the conviction that he can do so requires faith. But like all rational faith this too is not wishful thinking, but based upon the evidence of the past achievements of the human race and on the inner experience of each individual, on his own experience of reason and love.

While irrational faith is rooted in submission to a power which is felt to be overwhelmingly strong, omniscient and omnipotent, and in the abdication of one's own power and strength, rational faith is based upon the opposite experience. We have this faith in a thought because it is the result of our own observation and thinking. We have faith in the potentialities of others, of ourselves, and of mankind because, and only to the degree to which, we have experienced the growth of our own potentialities, the reality of growth in ourselves, the strength of our own power of reason and of love. *The basis of rational faith is productiveness;* to live by our faith means to live productively. It follows that the belief in power (in the sense of domination) and the use of power are the reverse of faith. To believe in power that exists is identical with disbelief in the growth of potentialities which are as yet unrealized. It is a prediction of the future based solely on the manifest present; but it turns out to be a grave miscalculation, profoundly irrational in its oversight of the human potentialities and human growth. There is no rational faith in power. There is submission to it or, on the part of those who have it, the wish to keep it. While to many power seems to be the most real of all things, the history of man has proved it to be the most unstable of all human achievements. Because of the fact that faith and power are mutually exclusive, all religions and political systems which originally are built on rational faith become corrupt and eventually lose what strength they have, if they rely on power or ally themselves with it.

To have faith requires *courage,* the ability to take a risk, the readiness even to accept pain and disappointment. Whoever insists on safety and security as primary conditions of life cannot have faith; whoever shuts himself off in a system of defense, where distance and possession are his means of security, makes himself a prisoner. To be loved, and to love, need courage, the courage to judge certain values as of ultimate concern—and to take the jump and stake everything on these values.

This courage is very different from the courage of which that famous braggart Mussolini spoke when he used the slogan "to live dangerously." His kind of courage is the courage of nihilism. It is rooted in a destructive attitude toward life, in the willingness to throw away life because one is incapable of loving it. The courage of despair is the opposite of the courage of love, just as the faith in power is the opposite of the faith in life.

Is there anything to be practiced about faith and courage? Indeed, faith can be practiced at every moment. It takes faith to bring up a child; it takes faith to fall asleep; it takes faith to begin any work. But we all are accustomed to having this kind of faith. Whoever does not have it suffers from overanxiety about his child, or from insomnia, or from the inability to do any kind of productive work; or he is suspicious, restrained from being close to anybody, or hypochondriacal, or unable to make any long-range plans. To stick to one's judgment about a person even if public opinion or some unforeseen facts seem to invalidate it, to stick to one's convictions even though they are unpopular—all this requires faith and courage. To take the difficulties, setbacks and sorrows of life as a challenge which to overcome makes us stronger, rather than as unjust punishment which should not happen to *us*, requires faith and courage.

The practice of faith and courage begins with the small details of daily life. The first step is to notice where and when one loses faith, to look through the rationalizations which are used to cover up this loss of faith, to recognize where one acts in a cowardly way, and again how one rationalizes it. To recognize how every betrayal of faith weakens one, and how increased weakness leads to new betrayal, and so on, in a vicious circle. Then one will also recognize that *while one is consciously afraid of not being loved, the real, though usually unconscious fear is that of loving.* To love means to commit oneself without guarantee, to give oneself completely in the hope that our love will produce love in the loved person. Love is an act of faith, and whoever is of little faith is also of little love. Can one say more about the practice of faith? Someone else might; if I were a poet or a preacher, I might try. But since I am not either of these, I cannot even try to say more about the practice of faith, but am sure that anyone who is really concerned can learn to have faith as a child learns to walk.

One attitude, indispensable for the practice of the art of loving, which thus far has been mentioned only implicitly should be discussed explicitly since it is basic for the practice of love: *activity*. I have said before that by activity is not meant "doing something," but an inner activity, the productive use of one's powers. Love is an activity; if I love, I am in a constant state of active concern with the loved person, but not only with him or her. For I shall become incapable of relating myself actively to the loved person if I am lazy, if I am not in a constant state of awareness, alertness, activity. Sleep is the only proper situation for inactivity; the state of awakeness is one in which laziness should have no place. The paradoxical situation with a vast number of people today is that they are half asleep when awake, and half awake when asleep, or when they want to sleep. To be fully awake is the condition for not being bored, or being boring—and indeed, not to be bored or boring is one of the main conditions for loving. To be active in thought, feeling, with one's eyes and ears, throughout the day, to avoid inner laziness, be it in the form of being receptive, hoarding, or plain wasting one's time, is an indispensable condition for the practice of the art of loving. It is an illusion to believe that one can separate life in such a way that one is productive in the sphere of love and unproductive in all other spheres. Productiveness does not permit of such a division of labor. The capacity to love demands a state of intensity, awakeness, enhanced vitality, which can only be the result of a productive and active orientation in many other spheres of life. If one is not productive in other spheres, one is not productive in love either.

The discussion of the art of loving cannot be restricted to the personal realm of acquiring and developing those characteristics and attitudes which have been described in this chapter. It is inseparably connected with the social realm. If to love means to have a loving attitude toward everybody, if love is a character trait, it must necessarily exist in one's relationship not only with one's family and friends, but toward those with whom one is in contact through one's work, business, profession. There is no "division of labor" between love for one's own and love for strangers. On the contrary, the condition for the existence of the former is the existence of the latter. To take this insight seriously means indeed a rather drastic change in one's social relations from the customary ones. While a great deal of lip service is paid to the religious ideal of love of one's neighbor, our relations are actually determined, at their best, by the principle of *fairness*. Fairness meaning not to use fraud and trickery in the exchange of commodities and services, and in the exchange of feelings. "I give you as much as you give me," in material goods as well as in love, is the prevalent ethical maxim in capitalist society. It may even be said that the development of fairness ethics is the particular ethical contribution of capitalist society.

The reasons for this fact lie in the very nature of capitalist society. In pre-capitalist societies, the exchange of goods was determined either by direct force, by tradition, or by personal bonds of love or friendship. In capitalism, the all-determining factor is the exchange on the market. Whether we deal with the commodity market, the labor market, or the market of services, each person exchanges whatever he has to sell for that which he wants to acquire under the conditions of the market, without the use of force or fraud.

Fairness ethics lend themselves to confusion with the ethics of the Golden Rule. The maxim "to do unto others as you would like them to do unto you" can be interpreted as meaning "be fair in your exchange with others." But actually, it was formulated originally as a more popular version of the Biblical "Love thy neighbor as thyself." Indeed, the Jewish-Christian norm of brotherly love is entirely different from fairness ethics. It means to love your neighbor, that is, to feel responsible for and one with him, while fairness ethics means *not* to feel responsible, and one, but distant and separate; it means to respect the rights of your neighbor, but not to love him. It is no accident that the Golden Rule has become the most popular religious maxim today; because it can be interpreted in terms of fairness ethics it is the one religious maxim which everybody understands and is willing to practice. But the practice of love must begin with recognizing the difference between fairness and love.

Here, however, an important question arises. If our whole social and economic organization is based on each one seeking his own advantage, if it is governed by the principle of egotism tempered only by the ethical principle of fairness, how can one do business, how can one act within the framework of existing society and at the same time practice love? Does the latter not imply giving up all one's secular concerns and sharing the life of the poorest? This question has been raised and answered in a radical way by the Christian monks, and by persons like Tolstoi, Albert Schweitzer, and Simone Weil. There are others[4] who share the opinion of the basic incompatibility between love and normal secular life within our society. They arrive at the result that to speak of love today means only to participate in the general fraud; they claim that only a martyr or a mad person can love in the world of today, hence that all discussion of love is nothing but preaching. This very respectable viewpoint lends itself readily to a rationalization of cynicism. Actually it is shared implicitly by the average person who feels "I would like to be a good Christian—but I would have to starve if I meant it seriously." This "radicalism" results in moral nihilism. Both the "radical thinkers" and the average person are unloving automatons and the only difference between them is that the latter is not aware of it, while the former knows it and recognizes the "historical necessity" of this fact.

I am of the conviction that the answer of the absolute incompatibility of love and "normal" life is correct only in an abstract sense. The *principle* underlying capitalistic society

\•

[4] Cf. Herbert Marcuse's article "The Social Implications of Psychoanalytic Revisionism," *Dissent,* New York, summer, 1955.

and the *principle* of love are incompatible. But modern society seen concretely is a complex phenomenon. A salesman of a useless commodity, for instance, cannot function economically without lying; a skilled worker, a chemist, or a physician can. Similarly, a farmer, a worker, a teacher, and many a type of businessman can try to practice love without ceasing to function economically. Even if one recognizes the principle of capitalism as being incompatible with the principle of love, one must admit that "capitalism" is in itself a complex and constantly changing structure which still permits of a good deal of non-conformity and of personal latitude.

In saying this, however, I do not wish to imply that we can expect the present social system to continue indefinitely, and at the same time to hope for the realization of the ideal of love for one's brother. People capable of love, under the present system, are necessarily the exceptions; love is by necessity a marginal phenomenon in present-day Western society. Not so much because many occupations would not permit of a loving attitude, but because the spirit of a production-centered, commodity-greedy society is such that only the non-conformist can defend himself successfully against it. Those who are seriously concerned with love as the only rational answer to the problem of human existence must, then, arrive at the conclusion that important and radical changes in our social structure are necessary, if love is to become a social and not a highly individualistic, marginal phenomenon. The direction of such changes can, within the scope of this book, only be hinted at.[5] Our society is run by a managerial bureaucracy, by professional politicians; people are motivated by mass suggestion, their aim is producing more and consuming more, as purposes in themselves. All

[5] In *The Sane Society*, Rinehart & Company, New York, 1955, I have tried to deal with this problem in detail.

activities are subordinated to economic goals, means have become ends; man is an automaton—well fed, well clad, but without any ultimate concern for that which is his peculiarly human quality and function. If man is to be able to love, he must be put in his supreme place. The economic machine must serve him, rather than he serve it. He must be enabled to share experience, to share work, rather than, at best, share in profits. Society must be organized in such a way that man's social, loving nature is not separated from his social existence, but becomes one with it. If it is true, as I have tried to show, that love is the only sane and satisfactory answer to the problem of human existence, then any society which excludes, relatively, the development of love, must in the long run perish of its own contradiction with the basic necessities of human nature. Indeed, to speak of love is not "preaching," for the simple reason that it means to speak of the ultimate and real need in every human being. That this need has been obscured does not mean that it does not exist. To analyze the nature of love is to discover its general absence today and to criticize the social conditions which are responsible for this absence. To have faith in the possibility of love as a social and not only exceptional-individual phenomenon, is a rational faith based on the insight into the very nature of man.

EPILOGUE
WORLD PERSPECTIVES

by Ruth Nanda Anshen

World Perspectives is dedicated to the concept of man born out of a universe perceived through a fresh vision of reality. Its aim is to present short books written by the most conscious and responsible minds of today. Each volume represents the thought and belief of each author and sets forth the interrelation of the changing religious, scientific, artistic, political, economic and social influences upon man's total experience.

This Series is committed to a re-examination of all those sides of human endeavor which the specialist was taught to believe he could safely leave aside. It interprets present and past events impinging on human life in our growing World Age and envisages what man may yet attain when summoned by an unbending inner necessity to the quest of what is most exalted in him. Its purpose is to offer new vistas in terms of world and human development while refusing to betray the intimate correlation between universality and in-

121

dividuality, dynamics and form, freedom and destiny. Each author treats his subject from the broad perspective of the world community, not from the Judaeo-Christian, Western or Eastern viewpoint alone.

Certain fundamental questions which have received too little consideration in the face of the spiritual, moral and political world crisis of our day, and in the light of technology which has released the creative energies of peoples, are treated in these books. Our authors deal with the increasing realization that spirit and nature are not separate and apart; that intuition and reason must regain their importance as the means of perceiving and fusing inner being with outer reality.

World Perspectives endeavors to show that the conception of wholeness, unity, organism is a higher and more concrete conception than that of matter and energy. Thus it would seem that science itself must ultimately pursue the aim of interpreting the physical world of matter and energy in terms of the biological conception of organism. An enlarged meaning of life, of biology, not as it is revealed in the test tube of the laboratory but as it is experienced within the organism of life itself is attempted in this Series. For the principle of life consists in the tension which connects spirit with the realm of matter. The element of life is dominant in the very texture of nature, thus rendering life, biology, a transempirical science. The laws of life have their origin beyond their mere physical manifestations and compel us to consider their spiritual source. In fact, the widening of the conceptual framework has not only served to restore order within the respective branches of knowledge, but has also disclosed analogies in man's position regarding the analysis and synthesis of experience in apparently separated domains of knowledge suggesting the possibility of an ever more embracing objective description of the meaning of life.

Knowledge, it is shown in these books, no longer consists in a manipulation of man and nature as opposite forces, nor in the reduction of data to mere statistical order, but is a means of liberating mankind from the destructive power of fear, pointing the way toward the goal of the rehabilitation of the human will and the rebirth of faith and confidence in the human person. The works published also endeavor to reveal that the cry for patterns, systems and authorities is growing less insistent as the desire grows stronger in both East and West for the recovery of a dignity, integrity and self-realization which are the inalienable rights of man who may now guide change by means of conscious purpose in the light of rational experience.

Other vital questions explored relate to problems of international understanding as well as to problems dealing with prejudice and the resultant tensions and antagonisms. The growing perception and responsibility of our World Age point to the new reality that the individual person and the collective person supplement and integrate each other; that the thrall of totalitarianism of both right and left has been shaken in the universal desire to recapture the authority of truth and of human totality. Mankind can finally place its trust not in a proletarian authoritarianism, not in a secularized humanism, both of which have betrayed the spiritual property right of history, but in a sacramental brotherhood and in the unity of knowledge. This new consciousness has created a widening of human horizons beyond every parochialism, and a revolution in human thought comparable to the basic assumption, among the ancient Greeks, of the sovereignty of reason; corresponding to the great effulgence of the moral conscience articulated by the Hebrew prophets;

analogous to the fundamental assertions of Christianity; or to the beginning of a new scientific era, the era of the science of dynamics, the experimental foundations of which were laid by Galileo in the Renaissance.

An important effort of this Series is to re-examine the contradictory meanings and applications which are given today to such terms as democracy, freedom, justice, love, peace, brotherhood and God. The purpose of such inquiries is to clear the way for the foundation of a genuine *world* history not in terms of nation or race or culture but in terms of man in relation to God, to himself, his fellow man and the universe that reach beyond immediate self-interest. For the meaning of the World Age consists in respecting man's hopes and dreams which lead to a deeper understanding of the basic values of all peoples.

Today in the East and in the West men are discovering that they are bound together, beyond any divisiveness, by a more fundamental unity than any mere agreement in thought and doctrine. They are beginning to know that all men possess the same primordial desires and tendencies; that the domination of man over man can no longer be justified by any appeal to God or nature; and such consciousness is the fruit of the spiritual and moral revolution, the great seismic upheaval, through which humanity is now passing.

World Perspectives is planned to gain insight into the meaning of man, who not only is determined by history but who also determines history. History is to be understood as concerned not only with the life of man on this planet but as including also such cosmic influences as interpenetrate our human world.

This generation is discovering that history does not conform to the social optimism of modern civilization and that the organization of human communities and the establishment of justice, freedom and peace are not only intellectual achievements but spiritual and moral achievements as well, demanding a cherishing of the wholeness of human personality and constituting a never-ending challenge to man, emerging from the abyss of meaninglessness and suffering, to be renewed and replenished in the totality of his life. "For as one's thinking is, such one becomes, and it is because of this that thinking should be purified and transformed, for were it centered upon truth as it is now upon things perceptible to the senses, who would not be liberated from his bondage."[1]

There is in mankind today a counterforce to the sterility and danger of a quantitative, anonymous mass culture, a new, if sometimes imperceptible, spiritual sense of convergence toward world unity on the basis of the sacredness of each human person and respect for the plurality of cultures. There is a growing awareness that equality and justice are not to be evaluated in mere numerical terms but that they are proportionate and analogical in their reality.

We stand at the brink of the age of the world in which human life presses forward to actualize new forms. The false separation of man and nature, of time and space, of freedom and security, is acknowledged and we are faced with a new vision of man in his organic unity and of history offering a richness and diversity of quality and majesty of scope hitherto unprecedented. In relating the accumulated wisdom of man's spirit to the new reality of the World Age, in articulating its thought and belief, *World Perspectives* seeks to encourage a renaissance of hope in society and of pride in man's decision as to what his destiny will be.

The vast extension of knowledge has led to a diminution of consciousness as a result of the tendency, due to some modern interpretations of science, to accept as the total

[1] *Maitri Upanishad* 6.34.4. 6.

truth only limited descriptions of truth. The triumphant advance of science, culminating in new realities concerning the subatomic world and overthrowing traditional assumptions of causality and uniformity, has almost succeeded in enfeebling man's faith in his spiritual and moral worth and in his own significance in the cosmic scheme. The experience of dread, into which contemporary man has been plunged through his failure to transcend his existential limits, is the experience of the problem of whether he shall attain to being through the knowledge of himself or shall not, whether he shall annihilate nothingness or whether nothingness shall annihilate him. For he has been forced back to his origins as a result of the atrophy of meaning, and his anabasis may begin once more through his mysterious greatness to re-create his life.

The suffering and hope of this century have their origin in the interior drama in which the spirit is thrust as a result of the split within itself, and in the invisible forces which are born in the heart and mind of man. This suffering and this hope arise also from material problems, economic, political, technological. History itself is not a mere mechanical unfolding of events in the center of which man finds himself as a stranger in a foreign land. The specific modern emphasis on history as progressive, the specific prophetic emphasis on God as acting through history, and the specific Christian emphasis on the historical nature of revelation must now surrender to the new history embracing the new cosmology—a profound event which is in the process of birth in the womb of that invisible universe which is the mind and heart of man. For our World Age is indeed the most dire and apocalyptic mankind has ever faced in all history, and the endeavor of *World Perspectives* is to point to that ultimate moral power at work in the universe, that very power upon which all human effort must at last depend.

This is the crisis in consciousness made articulate through the crisis in science. This is the new awakening after a long history which had its genesis in Descartes' denial that theology could exist as a science, on the one hand, and on the other, in Kant's denial that metaphysics could exist as a science. Some fossilized forms of such positivistic thinking still remain, manifesting themselves in a quasi-sociological mythology which, in the guise of scientific concepts, has generated a new animism resulting in a more primitive religion than the traditional faiths which it endeavors to replace. However, it is now conceded, out of the influences of Whitehead, Bergson and some phenomenologists that in addition to natural science with its tendency to isolate quantitative values there exists another category of knowledge wherein philosophy, utilizing its own instruments, is able to grasp the essence and innermost nature of the Absolute, of reality. The mysterious universe is now revealing to philosophy and to science as well an enlarged meaning of nature and of man which extends beyond mathematical and experimental analysis of sensory phenomena. This meaning rejects the mechanistic conception of the world and that positivistic attitude toward the world which considers philosophy as a kind of mythology adequate only for the satisfaction of emotional needs. In other words, the fundamental problems of philosophy, those problems which are central to life, are again confronting science and philosophy itself. Our problem is to discover a principle of differentiation and yet relationship lucid enough to justify and to purify both scientific and philosophical knowledge by accepting their mutual interdependence.

Justice itself which has been "in a state of pilgrimage and crucifixion" and now is slowly being liberated from the grip of social and political demonologies in the East as well as in the West, begins to question its own premises. Those modern revolutionary movements which have challenged the sacred institutions of society by protecting social injustice in the name of social justice are also being examined and reevaluated in *World Perspectives.*

When we turn our gaze retrospectively to the early cosmic condition of man in the third millennium, we observe that the concept of justice as something to which man has an inalienable right began slowly to take form and, at the time of Hammurabi in the second millennium, justice as inherently a part of man's nature and not as a beneficent gift to be bestowed, became part of the consciousness of society. This concept of human rights consisted in the demand for justice in the universe, a demand which exists also in the twentieth century through a curious analogy. In accordance with the ancient view, man could himself become a god, could assume the identity of the great cosmic forces in the universe which surrounded him. He could influence this universe, not by supplication, but by action. And now again this consciousness of man's harmonious relationship with the universe, with society and with his fellow men, can be actualized, and again not through supplication but through the deed.

Though never so powerful materially and technologically, Western democracy, with its concern for the sacredness of the human person gone astray, has never before been so seriously threatened, morally and spiritually. National security and individual freedom are in ominous conflict. The possibility of a universal community and the technique of degradation exist side by side. There is no doubt that evil is accumulated among men in their passionate desire for unity. And yet, confronted with this evil which had split, isolated and killed the living reality, confronted with death, man, from the very depths of his soul, cries out for "the unmediated whole of feeling and thought" and for the possibility to reassemble the fragments, to restore unity through justice. Christianity in history could only reply to this protest against evil by the Annunciation of the Kingdom, by the promise of Eternal Life—which demanded faith. But the spiritual and moral suffering of man had exhausted his faith and his hope. He was left alone. His suffering remained unexplained.

However, man has now reached the last extremity of denigration. He yearns to consecrate himself. And so, among the spiritual and moral ruins of the West and of the East a renaissance is prepared beyond the limits of nihilism, darkness and despair. In the depths of the Western and Eastern spiritual night, civilization with its many faces turning toward its source may rekindle its light in an imminent new dawn— even as in the last book of Revelation which speaks of a Second Coming with a new heaven, a new earth and a new religious quality of life.

> *And I saw a new heaven and a new*
> *earth: for the first heaven and the*
> *first earth were passed away. . . .*[2]

In spite of the infinite obligation of men and in spite of their finite power, in spite of the intransigence of nationalisms, and in spite of spiritual bereavement and moral amnesia, beneath the apparent turmoil and upheaval of the present, and out of the transformations of this dynamic period with the unfolding of a world-consciousness, the purpose of *World Perspectives* is to help quicken the "unshaken heart of well-rounded truth" and interpret the significant elements of the

[2]Revelation, 21:1.

World Age now taking shape out of the core of that un-dimmed continuity of the creative process which restores man to mankind while deepening and enhancing his communion with the universe.

Ruth Nanda Anshen
New York, 1956

ABOUT THE AUTHOR

Erich Fromm, born in Frankfurt, Germany, in 1900, received his Ph.D. degree from the University of Munich in the period 1923–24 and subsequently studied at the Psychoanalytic Institute in Berlin. Thereafter, until 1932, he worked in Frankfurt, both at the Psychoanalytic Institute there, where he was a lecturer, and at the Institute for Social Research at the University of Frankfurt.

From 1934 to 1939 Dr. Fromm was affiliated with the International Institute for Social Research in New York. In 1941 he joined the faculty of Bennington College, and was a guest lecturer at Columbia University, a Terry lecturer at Yale University, and a lecturer at the New School of Social Research in the following years. At the same time, he was Chairman of the Faculty of the William Alanson White Institute of Psychiatry, Psychoanalysis and Psychology, where he still lectures, while spending part of the year as a professor at the National University of Mexico.